S0-BBB-001

The Faithful Parent

The Faithful Parent

Discovering the Spirit of Purposeful Parenting

Seamus Carey

ROWMAN & LITTLEFIELD PUBLISHERS, INC.
Lanham • Boulder • New York • Toronto • Plymouth, UK

ROWMAN & LITTLEFIELD PUBLISHERS, INC.

Published in the United States of America
by Rowman & Littlefield Publishers, Inc.
A wholly owned subsidiary of The Rowman & Littlefield Publishing Group, Inc.
4501 Forbes Boulevard, Suite 200, Lanham, Maryland 20706
www.rowmanlittlefield.com

Estover Road
Plymouth PL6 7PY
United Kingdom

Copyright © 2007 by Rowman & Littlefield Publishers, Inc.

All rights reserved. No part of this publication may be reproduced,
stored in a retrieval system, or transmitted in any form or by any
means, electronic, mechanical, photocopying, recording, or otherwise,
without the prior permission of the publisher.

British Library Cataloguing in Publication Information Available

Library of Congress Cataloging-in-Publication Data:
Carey, Seamus, 1965–
  The faithful parent: discovering the spirit of purposeful parenting / Seamus
Carey.
      p. cm.
  Includes bibliographical references.
  ISBN-13: 978-0-7425-5858-8 (cloth : alk. paper)
  ISBN-10: 0-7425-5858-4 (cloth : alk. paper)
  ISBN-13: 978-0-7425-5859-5 (pbk. : alk. paper)
  ISBN-10: 0-7425-5859-2 (pbk. : alk. paper)
  1. Parenting—Philosophy. 2. Parenting—Religious aspects. 3. Parenting—Psy-
chological aspects. 4. Parent and child. I. Title.
  HQ755.8.C364 2007
  173—dc22   2007000368

Printed in the United States of America

♾™ The paper used in this publication meets the minimum requirements of
American National Standard for Information Sciences—Permanence of Paper
for Printed Library Materials, ANSI/NISO Z39.48-1992.

for my parents,
with deepest gratitude
for showing and sharing
your faith

Contents

Acknowledgments

There are several people who have contributed to this book in different ways, some by their critiques of early drafts of this work and others by their example. Kevin Curnin did both. I am always amazed at the clarity and insight with which he reads texts. His critiques are always direct and reveal potential that I would otherwise overlook. His questions and suggestions for early chapters of this book set the standard that I tried to maintain throughout. More importantly, many of the themes I write about in this book are descriptions of what I see he and his wife Ann Marie doing.

For the past fifteen years, Ferd Beck has been an invaluable friend and mentor. I hope that his mastery of the language is beginning to have an effect on my use of the language. Although a psychologist, Amelio D'Onofrio has provided the companionship of a philosopher, exploring and extending the ideas of great thinkers in casual conversation.

Jim Mustich's support and suggestions helped to make this book what it is and better than it would have been.

I am also incredibly fortunate for the colleagues I work with at Manhattan College, in particular, Rentaro Hashimoto, who makes working in the philosophy department a constant pleasure.

Roger Gottlieb has been a mentor, and friend, and an example of courage and insight for the past ten years. As usual, his comments and suggestions made substantial improvements to this book.

I am thankful to neighbors and friends in my community where I witness loving, concerned parenting every day. I am especially grateful to Janine Bastone who took the time to read early drafts of this work and posed challenging questions to help refine my thinking.

Finally, my family: Noreen, Caitriona, Anna, and James— to say thank you is inadequate for the indescribable joy you give me every day.

A version of Chapter 1 appeared in *Philosophical Practice*, Vol. 2, No. 2, Summer 2006, under the title "Philosophical Faith and the Activities of Parenting."

PHILOSOPHICAL FAITH OR THE FAITH WE ALREADY HAVE

There is a strange paradox at work in contemporary America concerning the issue of faith. On the one hand, talk of religious faith has become mainstream. The president has declared that his faith inspires him and helps him to govern the country. On national television, professional athletes genuflect to pray with their teammates and their opponents at the end of games. Millions of working Americans flock to megachurches throughout the country giving themselves over to the charismatic words of their preachers. And many of the most forceful advocates for family life proclaim that a healthy family depends on a strong religious faith.

Given the prevalence of faith talk, it might seem out of place to argue that parents and families need a revival of faith in order to successfully address the challenges they face in today's world. And yet, this book will argue that a major source of suffering among parents and their children is a lack of faith. But I write in this instance as a philosopher, as one shaped by the tradition of Plato, not Abraham, though there is much for the philosopher to learn from the father of religious faith. The faith that I am arguing for is not a faith in God, yet it does not preclude religious faith. Instead, I am arguing for the nurturing of a multivalent prereligious, worldly faith. As the expression of religious faith seems to be on the rise, philosophical faith, as we will present it, is eroding from our lives and the strength of parents and families is eroding with it. While a healthy religious faith can benefit individuals, their families, and society as a whole, the evidence suggests it is not enough to adequately support the healthy development of parents and their children in today's world.

Beneath the increasingly public expression of faith, the standards and trends of popular culture are eating away at the fabric of family life and the healthy development of children. Religious faith, on its own, seems powerless to stop it. The religious promise of salvation does little for parents who are trying to decide how to help their daughter overcome an eating disorder or advise their son on how to respond to being bullied at school. It doesn't help them decide which specialist to see when their child has a rare physical disorder, or where to live in the face of escalating real estate prices, or how to handle the burden of rising college tuition. Religious faith can be a source of strength for parents, but parents need more. They need a faith that will provide resolve and insight to address the pressing concerns of everyday life, as they occur. They need to supplement their faith in the promise of heaven with a faith in something closer to home. Without the philosophical faith for which I am arguing, parents, children, families, and society will continue to struggle to identify and accomplish what they need in order to flourish.

Philosophical faith, for those who have it, is a subtle source of strength, a sixth sense that helps us to navigate the treacherous waters of contemporary life with insight and conviction. It is akin to the intuitive insight that we enjoy as a result of sound reflection on our lives and our place in the world. Philosophical faith is patient and quiet. It recognizes that those things that are worthwhile in a fulfilling life often happen slowly and with little or no announcement. Philosophical faith is also complex and difficult. There are many obstacles to overcome in order to find this faith and to enjoy its benefits. Despite the obstacles, however, there is nothing more important to effective parenting and healthy family life than philosophical faith at the outset of the twenty-first century.

Philosophical faith is not a substitute for religious faith. Although different, these two avenues of faith share essential characteristics. The most significant differences arise out of their divergent points of focus. The primary focus of religious faith is the relationship between human beings and a mysterious God that is beyond this world and beyond human comprehension. This relationship is forever asymmetrical and it is punctuated by worship. Philosophical faith, on the other hand, begins much closer to home with a faith in oneself: in understanding and acting on one's principles and beliefs. Philosophical faith moves out from a faith in oneself to include a faith in the world, that is, a faith that there is some order, meaning, and intelligibility to the world. For parents, this faith includes faith in our children, in their ability to learn and to appreciate the need for sacrifice, to overcome adversity, and to resist those things that are detrimental to their well-being.

Faith in oneself, faith in the world, and faith in children are the first three dimensions of philosophical faith. There are two others: faith in reason and faith in faith itself. Reason is the faculty that enables us to decipher order and meaning in an often chaotic world. When used correctly, reason is powerful; but we will enjoy its benefits only if we begin with a belief in its power. And finally, we need to believe that it is worthwhile to develop all of these dimensions of faith if we are to make the changes necessary to live in accordance with our own beliefs and principles, to enjoy the strength that comes from having faith in ourselves.

Philosophical faith is not something that we can create and implant in people or society, nor do we need to. In calling for a rejuvenation of philosophical faith, it is critical to recognize that such a faith is already in place. That is, we rely on philosophical faith all the time in making our way through the world.[1] For instance, it is with a profound faith in themselves, in nature, and in the world that new parents take those first steps outside the hospital door with their newborn infant. The newest, most important concern in their lives is also the most vulnerable. They trust themselves to care for the infant properly, even if they have yet to figure out all of the details. They trust that nature will run a favorable course and enable the infant to get stronger each day. They trust that the world, with all of its unexpected contingencies, will not throw a speeding car in their way as they drive home.

There are many other examples of how we rely on philosophical faith. In fact, we rely on this faith for almost everything we do. For instance, the surgeon enters the operating room with a faith in his ability to respond to whatever he finds upon opening the patient. We take it on faith that other drivers stop at red lights, that the food we eat is not poisoned, and that we can successfully walk down the stairs without falling. If we stopped to consider how the body makes its way down a flight of stairs rather than taking it on faith as we usually do, it would become a much more difficult task, possibly leading to a fall. If we had no faith in the reliability of our fellow drivers on the road, we would be paralyzed out of fear and likely cause many accidents. Nobody would want a surgeon that lacks faith in his abilities. And if new parents had no faith, they would never leave the hospital. So unlike religious faith, which involves a life conversion for those who lack it, philosophical faith is already at work in our lives. By increasing our awareness of it, however, we can strengthen and refine it, making it a positive and central force in our lives as parents.

To suggest that driving or walking down a flight of stairs is an act of faith might seem offensive to those who are accustomed to thinking of faith in religious terms. Abraham, the father of religious faith, and the father of Isaac, had much bigger concerns to resolve with his faith. One cannot come away from reading Kierkegaard's analysis of the Abraham story without what he describes as fear and trembling. Kierkegaard makes it clear that the stakes in religious faith are immense, life and death in fact, whereas walking down steps or driving a car seems less important. And yet, despite the differences between the religious faith of Abraham and the philosophical faith we are seeking to rejuvenate, there are deep structural similarities. For instance, a parent's sense of self and self-worth, a parent's faith in her child and in the hidden meaning and coherence of the world, as well as faith in the outcome of cultivating a faith in self and world are all a part of religious faith. Consider Abraham's circumstances. God's command was so unique, Abraham could not discuss it with anyone to get support or comfort. His sense of self, his ego, was not going to receive any affirmation from his family, friends, or the accepted norms of society. He was alone. In his isolation, he had to have faith in himself. He had to know that he was not psychotic, even though his relationship with God was not rational. He had to have an unshakeable confidence that his faculties were working correctly in deciding what to do. Like Abraham, parents can often feel isolated, alone, and misunderstood, as if our family and our entire community are on a different page, valuing different things. In order to make good decisions in these circumstances, we need to have faith in ourselves, as Abraham did, even if our faith does not involve hearing the voice of God. Although the source of a parent's dilemmas and concerns are different today, Abraham remains an ally, showing us the depths of human courage and the resolve of self-reliance in the face of the most difficult circumstances.

In addition to faith in one's self, sound parenting also requires faith in the meaning and structure of the world. The search for meaning and an underlying principle or structure to the world has been a central part of philosophical thought from the beginning. The first philosophers forged a new way of thinking when they looked to nature rather than mythological gods to explain what was happening in the world. In searching for rational explanations about the ways of the world, the first philosophers also relied on faith. For instance, they relied on a faith that the hidden principles and structure of nature could be known. Like the first philosophers and those who have followed their lead, parents rely on a faith in the meaning and structure of the world that is not always apparent in the routines of daily life. Out of the unpredictability and confusion of life with children, we hope for epiphanies of meaning, order, and coherence. When a child is sick, we trust in the healing forces of nature to make him better. When we do not understand or approve of their behavior at various stages of their development, we believe in their future and what they will become. We rely on our faith in nature or the world more than we know, and by increasing our awareness of this faith, we can strengthen our resolve as parents by giving ourselves a broader, deeper, and more meaningful context to make sense of our children's lives and our relationships with them. The primary context in which parents understand themselves and their children is the family. In those dark, contentious, thankless moments, when family life feels like a prison, parents can benefit from their faith in the family structure as the best environment for achieving our highest fulfillment.

As most parents quickly realize, children are worlds unto themselves. Just as we rely on our faith in nature or the world and structures within the world, we also rely on our faith in children. Even when there seems to be no rhyme or reason to a child's development, we often find ourselves trusting in the fact that there is deep and important meaning in his behavior. We can also have faith in the abilities of children to adapt to the world, to overcome obstacles, to learn and grow from hardship and suffering. This dimension of faith is bolstered by the ever-deepening insights of science and medicine into the workings of nature, especially with regard to the human body. But no matter how insightful and powerful science and medicine become, they cannot eliminate the mystery that resides at the core of (human) existence. The more science reveals, the more mysterious and more majestic the ways of nature appear. We can live and work with this mystery as a source of strength if we give it sufficient time to occupy our minds. The paradox of the simultaneous deepening of mystery with increasing knowledge draws us closer to the faith that rises at the interplay of both; in particular, our faith in the abilities of children and their parents to adapt to an ever-changing world.

While there are millennia of philosophical debate and dialogue concerning the relationship between faith and reason, we have too often taken for granted the importance of faith *in* reason. It is widely understood that faith and reason work together in the pursuit of knowledge and human wisdom, especially in religious contexts. But the initial movement of any rational inquiry is the belief that reason is capable and useful. The world of children, and the families of which they are a part, is very often an irrational world. Children write on newly painted walls, teenagers abuse their bodies, siblings express their insecurities by treating each other with disdain. Reasonable behavior is not the common denominator in these all too familiar situations. And so often our response as parents mirrors the irrational behavior. Reason has a sneaky tendency to abandon us in the heat of the moment leaving our spontaneous responses to be driven by heated emotions. And yet, reason is our most powerful and most cherished human faculty. Reason gives us hope, the virtue that combats despair, because reason makes it possible for adults to step back from habitual, emotionally charged situations to respond with insight and wisdom. In other words, reason makes change, substantive and lasting change, possible in family life.

Finally, our rehabilitation of philosophical faith for parents will focus on the dimension of faith that is required in order for one to begin a process of healthy self-development. This is the part of faith wherein one trusts in the fact that it is worthwhile to endure difficulty and hardship for the sake of a better life that is not yet known. This dimension of faith plays at least two critical roles in effective parenting and another in a child's development. For parents this faith is necessary, first, because it is easy and dangerous to substitute the mechanical processes of caring for children for the work we need to do with ourselves if we are to continue to develop and grow as healthy and mature adults. Second, it is critical for parents if they are to make difficult but wise choices for, and demands on, their children. It will enable parents to say "no" to children, even when it means creating temporary conflict in the home. It will also give parents the resolve to defend and support their children when no one else will. This dimension of faith also benefits children directly because, by allowing children to endure difficult situations, to take responsibility for their actions, even when it is painful, parents allow them to find and develop their own resolve, their own character, which is critical if children are to grow into healthy adults. Lastly, this dimension of faith is essential for parents to be able to see alternatives to their parenting styles. Without the faith that alternatives are possible and that they are worthwhile, parents will remain stuck in their established patterns of thinking and acting. The final dimension of faith, then, is a source of parental autonomy and freedom.

One who develops a mature character and a capacity for thinking clearly will discover things about the world that are not obvious to an undeveloped self. But standards of popular culture do not encourage such development. This lack of encouragement makes it critical for parents to have faith that it is worth engaging in the difficult work of self-development for themselves and for their children. Whereas Abraham trusted that God would restore his life, philosophical faith trusts that the world, and the cultivation of our capacities for understanding the world, will provide a life for which it is worth sacrificing much of what is available on the surface of everyday life. Unfortunately, this faith, in all of its dimensions is eroding from our families and communities. This erosion is often difficult to detect because it is happening behind the activities of well-intentioned parents.

The vast majority of parents are trying to do what is best when it comes to caring for their children. Philosophical faith is a means of supporting, guiding, and developing a better understanding of how to best fulfill these intentions. Unless we examine our lives as parents, our motivations and our methods, we are likely to be led astray by the expectations and demands of society. Social conformity rarely serves our children well, and when it does, it is usually a short-term benefit. By developing philosophical faith, parents will be empowered to search for, and live by, the values they believe in most. They will be able to retain an awareness of both short-term and long-term goals, without sacrificing one for the other.

Philosophical faith is nourished by moments of silence and stillness. By honoring the self with significant periods of silence and stillness, parents can cultivate a disposition, an *ethos*, of composure to address the most difficult and the most enjoyable situations with insight and wisdom. It is impossible that a parent be composed in all situations. But a healthy philosophical faith will also enable a parent to recognize and rely on the resilience of children to recover from and over-come the words and deeds we regret as parents. This dimension of faith is not a license to treat children without care, respect, and composure, but it does provide parents with some room to accept their imperfections.

As the stoic philosopher Epicurus declared centuries ago, "Empty is the philosophical argument by which no human suffering is alleviated. For just as there is no use in medicine, unless it casts out the illness of bodies, so too there is no use in philosophy, unless it casts out suffering from the soul." This book is intended to help parents to minimize the suffering in family life and to find fulfillment, strength, and resolve as they guide their children toward healthy adulthood. As with anything that is worthwhile in life, this is a difficult task. Hence, it is helpful to remind ourselves that we are not alone in this journey. We are the beneficiaries of ancient and profound wisdom from both secular and spiritual traditions. We will appeal to the spokesmen of these traditions for encouragement and guidance in the search for our own source of faithful strength. We will draw upon the example of Abraham and Plato as well as their spiritual and intellectual descendants in sorting through the distractions and the resources the world provides us. In their example, we will see that human beings not only can, but must transcend the confines of unreflective, mundane human existence. For parents seeking to do the best for their children, while also searching for some higher meaning and purpose for their own lives, this is not only welcome news, it is a requisite journey.

Note

1. In *The Visible and the Invisible*, French phenomenologist Maurice Merleau-Ponty develops the concept of perceptual faith as a necessary precursor to scientific knowledge. In discussing philosophical faith, I am expanding the meaning of Merleau-Ponty's notion of perceptual faith to apply to areas of our life beyond scientific inquiry.

CHAPTER ONE

FAITH IN THE HIGHER SELF

The first dimension of philosophical faith begins with faith in one's self. Faith in one's self has two distinct parts: faith in one's *capacities* for accessing or understanding the ideas of the higher self, and faith in the *content* of those ideas. Along with faith in the world, especially the world of children, and faith in the worthiness of developing these dimensions of faith, faith in the self is eroding from the lives of parents and it is affecting children and communities. This erosion can be difficult to detect because it often happens behind the veil of highly successful parents who are competent and confident in so many areas of their lives. And yet, there are numerous examples from community activities that can be interpreted as a parent's loss of faith in self.

I recently witnessed a few examples of an erosion of faith at local childhood sporting events. As I understand it, childhood sports can provide a number of benefits for children. They get exercise. They meet new friends. They challenge themselves to improve at what they are doing. They learn to compete, which means learning to win and lose. Some learn that they want to pursue a sport seriously, while others learn that sports are not their thing. Generations of children have gained invaluable insights about themselves, friends, competition, fairness, and sacrifice as a result of playing sports.

I wasn't thinking of all the ramifications of participating in sports when I went to the first couple of softball games that my daughter was playing. At the first game I went to, I sat in the outfield taking in the sun while the coaches patiently guided girls to positions on the field and showed them how to hold the bat. Two or three girls on each team were capable of hitting the ball as far as an infielder, while the rest swung aimlessly at the ball rarely making contact. As the time passed, I noticed that I wasn't the only one that had some difficulty staying interested in the game. Two girls who were playing on the infield had congregated at second base with their baseball gloves on one hand and sticks in the other. They were both on one knee making pictures in the dirt. Another pair walked with their backs to the game as they talked, seemingly having forgotten about the game entirely. With increasing frequency, coaches and parents had to remind their daughters to "pay attention" and "get ready to catch the ball." These reminders became less and less effective as the game wore on.

As I watched the scene unfold, I couldn't help thinking about the usefulness of these games. It didn't seem as though the girls were being challenged or that they were even learning anything about the game. They were getting no exercise and the friends they congregated with were most often girls they already knew from school. It seemed to be an innocuous foray into the world of sport and I couldn't help wondering how the girls felt about the game. After the novelty of wearing a uniform wore off, it seemed as though there was little that the girls could find appealing, other than socializing with their friends. After all, they could draw figures in the dirt anywhere and they wouldn't have to be interrupted by adults telling them to do something else.

These thoughts occurred toward the end of the hour or so that the game lasted until I heard a coach yell, "last batter." I was relieved and stood up to begin walking toward the bench to get my daughter and bring her to the car. As I walked closer to the field, I noticed a new urgency among the girls that wasn't there for any other part of the game. The girls seemed attentive. They were all facing the batter and ready to move. The batter hit the ball along the ground and the coaches and parents yelled "run, keep running." The girl who hit the ball ran around the infield touching all four bases while a few girls in the field chased the ball, not sure what to do with it once it was picked it up. At the instant the batter jumped on home plate, one of the girls in the field stretched her arms straight into the air and yelled with great enthusiasm, "donut time!" With this announcement the players on both teams broke into a full sprint to their respective benches where there was a parent waiting with a box of Dunkin Donuts.

The first time a game concluded with "donut time," I thought it was a special occasion, perhaps a birthday party. But after the second and third time I became alarmed. As softball season turned to soccer season, I was dismayed. It turns out that at every soccer game in our community, for children's games that last one hour, a parent is assigned to bring a snack. These snacks can be donuts, but usually they are some kind of chips like Doritos and a sugar drink. Sometimes these snacks come in a variety pack, which leads children to seek out their favorite snack early in the game and hold it throughout, frequently checking to make sure it is where they left it while they play.

Lately, I have been encouraged by some parents who bring healthy snacks, though I am not sure why children need to be fed while at an event that lasts only one hour. More importantly, there is a larger trend at work here. Children are turning up to games with confusing messages as to why they are there and what the value of participating is. For example, at a recent soccer game, a mother was excitedly following the game up and down the sideline. Realizing that she had walked closely in front of me, she politely said, "excuse me," and explained that she gets excited because she "loves these games so much." She was encouraging her daughter who was more interested in something on the sidelines than in the game. In fact, while the mother was standing next to me, her daughter sprinted off the field as the ball was coming toward the goal she was defending. The mother ran after her, picked her up and placed her back in the position she was playing. As the daughter again looked to the sideline, away from the action, the mother told her, "if you stay there, I will get you the toy you've been asking for." The daughter immediately stopped ignoring her mother and responded, "You mean the doll." And the mother responded, "yes." The little girl turned and ran toward the play.

The parents in these stories are well intentioned, but they demonstrate a loss of philosophical faith. That is, in feeling the need to supplement a sporting event with donuts or a toy, they reveal a loss of faith in themselves, in the ability of games to be enjoyed by children, in their children's ability to find that enjoyment, and even if they can't, to learn from participating, and finally, they have lost faith that it is worthwhile to resist the conventions that have crept into these activities. Parents can reverse these trends and the negative effects that follow from them by understanding and recovering the philosophical faith that is eroding. To begin this recovery, parents can focus on faith in one's self, which underlies the other dimensions of faith. And while this faith is not equivalent to religious faith, it can be understood as a part of it. Let us briefly consider Abraham's circumstances to see why.

Abraham, Plato, and Faith in Self

For me, one of the most gut-wrenching parts of the Abraham story in the Old Testament book of *Genesis* is the thought of Isaac asking his father on the way to Mount Moriah, "Father, . . . where is the lamb for the burnt offering?" Abraham can't or won't give him the answer he must fear is true, and instead replied, "my son, God himself will provide the lamb for the burnt offering" (Wansbrough, 1990). As a parent, I can't help wondering if this response is a cop-out, one that I often take when I say to my five-year-old son, "we'll see" when he asks for something I don't want him to have in order to avoid the crying that is sure to follow a direct denial. Or worse, is Abraham's deferral an act of cowardice, withholding the truth from his son (and wife Sarah)? Is he trying to preserve Isaac's respect for him a little longer, knowing that if he told his son the truth, Isaac couldn't love him? How could a son love a father who was going to kill him? Or is it, as most have regarded it, an act of unfathomable courage? Is Abraham trying to protect Isaac and to preserve his respect for God, knowing that if he told him that God is demanding this sacrifice, Isaac could no longer love God? This is a troubling story, not just for parents, but for all aspiring believers.

To have faith in God means that one cannot hold anything or anyone higher than God, even a beloved child. This is the first commandment. Only God is God. The stakes of religious faith are clear and they are ultimate. One must be willing to sacrifice everything to obey or follow God's command. But Abraham is the father of faith not only because he was willing to sacrifice Isaac, but also because he had faith in God that he would somehow get Isaac back. Abraham's faith is remarkable because he believes that in spite of making it impossible to have Isaac to love and protect as a son if he killed him, he would have Isaac, because with God all things are possible. In the face of the absurd, as Kierkegaard puts it, Abraham believes God will not only provide him with what he needs but that his life will be full.

Abraham also teaches us that faith is lonely. The call from God is madness to those who are reasonable, those who do not hear what God has to say. It is incomprehensible and incommunicable. He cannot tell his wife Sarah or run it by his friends to weigh the pros and cons of such an act. They will not understand. They did not receive the call. He must carry this burden alone without the reinforcement of social or family approval. There are no support groups, no therapist to bolster the ego when it comes to answering God's call. He cannot explain to Isaac or anyone else that God's command is above all and that Isaac is second to God. They would not understand. Abraham has leaped out of the realm of reason. His act of faith is unethical if ethics is understood as that which makes sense and applies to all universally. As Kierkegaard argues, the individual who responds to the call of God is higher than the group, above the universal, beyond ethics.[1] This is an awesome burden and it is madness to the reasonable. To those who aspire to have faith, Abraham is courageous and humble. He has the courage to walk alone trusting that he is not delusional, even if he is mad when measured against the standards of rationality. Abraham trusts in himself that it is indeed God who is calling and that he is not psychotic.

Abraham sets a standard for faith that is beyond reasonable parents who are trying to protect, nurture, and guide their children toward a healthy adult life. Most parents are not tuned into the voice of God. In fact, many of the parents I know have a hard time accepting critiques of their children from schoolteachers, much less make them sacrifice for God. And yet, Abraham's willingness to stand alone, outside the conventions of society, to trust in his capacities, and to sacrifice the life he had for something unknown are qualities we all need to be effective parents. The strength that comes from faith is what enables parents to resist unhealthy choices for their children like bringing donuts to athletic events in order to fit in. It is not only the life of religious faith that requires these qualities. Parents require it also. And in a nonreligious context, Plato reinforces the importance of these qualities for anyone who wants to achieve beyond social convention.

Plato's Ship

In Book VI of the *Republic*, Plato presents a timeless psychological analysis of the person who seeks to go beyond social norms. He begins with a parable about a ship, its captain, and the crew that wants to overthrow him. In this parable, Plato depicts the captain as one whose faculties are failing, rendering him ineffective at guiding the ship. The crew splinters into rival factions as they see the captain's failing faculties as an opportunity to seize control of the ship. Taking control of the ship becomes an exercise in power without any regard for the navigational expertise that is required of an effective sea captain. As this power struggle develops, there is one person on the ship who spends his time alone, away from the crowds, studying the stars. He is the one person that is qualified to navigate the ship but he has no interest in fighting for power.

Plato, of course, is describing a familiar political situation in which those with resources and power hold office and lead societies, even if they are not qualified to do so. Plato reminds his readers that we should not expect the one who is qualified to chase power just as we don't expect a doctor to seek out the sick. Unfortunately, societies fail to recognize the qualities of a good leader and their need to be led by highly qualified leaders. As a result, good leaders are most often ignored. And like the sick person who does not seek out the right doctor, societies that choose the wrong leaders suffer.

In his analysis of the parable, Plato reminds us that those who spend their time seeking the truth, seeking expertise, are often isolated while the masses struggle for power. Just as Abraham's answer to God's call renders him alone among his peers, the philosopher who pursues truth is often alone. And worse, the path to truth is fraught with painful obstacles. Plato points out those who are willing to pursue truth are rare. When such a person comes along, those in positions of influence try to persuade him to join them. They do so by offering the aspiring philosopher praise, honor, and riches, tempting him with the goods of society. Only the very special can resist such temptation, and for the one who does, the pursuit of truth becomes even more difficult. Those who are unsuccessful in luring the philosopher with praise and honor will turn on him. He will hear criticism and ridicule, often from those who are closest, even family. This criticism usually takes the form of questions such as, "what good is studying philosophy," "that's a waste of time," or more bluntly "that's stupid." Only the convinced, the resolute, those hungry for truth will overcome these painful barbs. And when they do, they will often feel alone in the world.

Like the story of Abraham, this story reminds us of the difficulty entailed in trying to move beyond social conventions. It warns of the alienation that accompanies a thoughtful life. It points to the possibility that those who are closest to us, including family, might be threatened by such a life. For parents, these difficulties are magnified since they are faced with pressures from both their children and their peers. Many parents find this pressure to be overwhelming and it leads them to follow the lead of the community unreflectively. They end up making decisions based on what others do and expect rather than what they might come to know from their own better judgment, their own ideas,[2] if they learned to listen for them. It is an age-old question why we choose in this way, why we sacrifice living a life that is true to one's self, or why we sometimes sacrifice the healthy development of children for the sake of social acceptance. We usually blame regrettable choices on a lack of resolve.

The resolve of Abraham or Plato's philosopher is rare but when it is found it is always hitched upon the shoulders of faith: faith that the ideals of truth and justice and authenticity are real; that enduring the difficulties that come with pursuing such a life is worthwhile; and more simply, a faith that one has the capacity to know these ideals and to live in accordance with them. To find the resolve that is required to be an extraordinary parent, we need to uncover this faith, which is quickly eroding in our communities.

Emerson's Genius

As parents, we are entrusted to guide our children toward a healthy adult life. We try to teach and demonstrate the skills that are necessary to be successful as workers, friends, parents, and citizens. At first glance, it may be hard to see what we have to learn from Abraham's approach to parenting. We can't be sufficiently focused on guiding children toward healthy adulthood if we're thinking about sacrificing them at the alter. Abraham was not a model citizen, husband, or father because his actions went beyond the universal, beyond ethics, beyond social norms. And yet, it is in going beyond these conventions that makes Abraham great.

Almost all philosophers would agree with Abraham and Plato that one must go beyond the conventions of social norms in order to achieve greatness. But as simple as this sounds, it is difficult to achieve. We have seen that one reason such a move is so difficult is that society offers many temptations, especially to the talented. The attempts to allure the seeker appeal to the predominant part of the self, the part of the self that we rely on and pay attention to most of the time, the ego-self. This is the part of the self that is formed, affirmed, and threatened by social norms. It is the ego-self that absorbs the messages that the world has to offer telling one who and what he is and should be. It is the part of our identity that is shaped in relationship with the world, especially the world of family and friends. This part of the self has a powerful tendency to look around, peering side to side, to see what the neighbor, the coworker, or the child's classmates are doing in order to compare accomplishments. This is the part of us that decides to bring donuts to a child's game, knowing that it is unhealthy because we are concerned about fitting in. Being accepted, honored, or praised is how the ego-self measures its worth. And while the ego-self is essential for making our way through the world, for executing everyday transactions necessary for survival, there is no greatness here. Greatness lies in putting the ego-self in its place and moving beyond to a higher or deeper self. The call to move beyond the ego-self is almost universal among philosophers. This move they share with Abraham's dramatic transcendence of the ego and the conventions that might have supported it.

The faith that such a move is possible is the first dimension of philosophical faith. The belief, without any assurances from our usual social crutches, that there is a dimension of the self that is beyond and bigger than the ego, is where faith begins. This is the higher self that Emerson refers to as Genius. Genius, for Emerson, is not a function of IQ. It is a matter of belief. He writes, "to *believe* your own thought, to *believe* that what is true for you in your private heart is true for all men—that is genius" (Emerson, 1984, p. 175, emphasis added).

But belief in one's own ideas, the ideas in "one's private heart" that constitutes genius is already moving past the first dimension of philosophical faith. The first dimension is simply the belief that we are capable of having such ideas. Emerson makes it clear that these ideas serve us better as a measure of well-being than do social conventions when he writes, "society everywhere is in conspiracy against the manhood of everyone of its members. . . . Society is a joint-stock company, in which the members agree, for the better securing of his bread to each shareholder, to surrender the liberty and culture of the eater. The virtue in most requests is conformity. Self-reliance is its aversion" (Emerson, 1984, p. 178). If we fail to believe that we are capable of finding a measure beyond social conformity and acceptance, not only can we never find the content of our own genius, we cannot be our own person, as adults and parents need to be.

We tend to think of peer pressure as a concern for adolescence, and yet, when we observe the behavior of adults and parents, we realize that the effects of peer pressure are not easily left behind. These pressures can cause us to seriously doubt or forget our capacity for great ideas. When this doubt settles in, the ego loses its footing in the higher self. It becomes detached from that part of the self that can access the ideas that move us to find and forge unique paths in life. When the ego loses anchor in the higher self, it looks elsewhere for affirmation. It looks to the arbitrary winds of praise, honor, power, and status. These are the fast foods, the caffeine buzz that gives unhealthy nourishment and stimulation to the ego. Like the drug addict whose days are programmed around finding the next fix, the ego can become fixated on these external sources of affirmation, orienting its entire life around receiving them. When this occurs, the first dimension of philosophical faith is effectively smothered. The measure of greatness is lost, replaced by the external measure of social conformity and acceptance. Genius becomes something for other people to achieve because one loses the touch with the source of his own genius. For parents, this translates into signing the children up for the next activity because that is what the neighbors are doing. It means bribing a child to pay attention to a soccer game because the parent loves it or buying the newest video game or gadget because it is what other kids have. And over time, it means teaching children to lose touch with the source of their own genius.

So becoming a faithful parent begins with the belief that each of us has a higher self that can never be satisfied by merely measuring up to social standards. It recognizes that we all have our own genius and that we are all capable of being great parents. This is a subtle but critical dimension of faith that makes it possible to realize the richer dimensions of faith that build upon it. Without the faith in one's capacity to access a higher self, there will be no search, no work undertaken to develop one's self or to demand the difficult work of children that builds character. With this faith in place, however, parents can build on it and cultivate a faith in the ideas of the higher self, the ideas of one's own genius.

Faith in the Content of the Higher Self

Faith in the higher self or one's genius is more than just faith in the capacity to access the higher self. Faith in the higher self also involves trusting in the *content* of the higher mind, the mind that extends beyond the ideas of the ego. By extending beyond the limits and interests of the ego-self, we find that the ideas of the higher self are not generated exclusively by the self. As a result, the more attuned we become to the higher self, the less concerned we are with the ego-self, the self that we are so often identified with. When we are attuned to the higher self, we move toward and, in turn, are moved by the world beyond the ego-self. In order to heed the ideas of the higher self, we must sacrifice the ego's desire for control. The ideas of the higher self always come to us in excess. They are too much for the conceptual apparatus or the categories of the ego to contain or control. The excess of these ideas are power-ful. When we pay attention to the excess of our ideas it can move us but not always with any clear direction. This excess jolts us out of the ordinary everyday mindset with which we are so used to seeing the world, but these ideas do not often tell us the next move. In pulling us back from the everyday, the ideas of the higher self force us to proceed with our eyes and ears wide open searching for clues, for direction. In order to be moved by these higher ideas, however, the chattering voice of the ego needs to be silenced so that the ideas of the higher self can be heard. For parents, this is difficult because it means finding quiet time and space away from the ever-present needs of children and the weight of constant demands that come with belonging to communities. To find ideas by which parents want to direct their lives and the lives of their children is a challenge, which is followed by the challenge of living in accordance with the ideas that are revealed to us.

In searching for these ideas, it is helpful to know where one should be looking. It is slightly misleading to refer to the mind that is bigger than the ego as "higher." We know from neurophysiology that the more sophisticated processes of reason are housed in specific parts of the brain such as the neocortex. These processes allow us to analyze and sort information, to understand and communicate language, and to remember past events both long term and short term. The functions of the brain are highly complex and out of this complexity, the analytical mind and the ego-self are formed. The higher self, however, goes beyond the analytical mind. As powerful as the analytical mind is, it cannot account for the power of genius, which Emerson argues is divinely inspired. The wisdom of genius is felt and processed by the body, not just the brain. The higher self is literally felt by the lower portions of the body where moods, emotions, feelings are experienced. These ideas have the power to move us, to change the direction of our lives, if we develop the capacity to hear them. By listening to the feelings, emotions, and moods of the body we learn what our deepest needs are. For instance, when the body gets tired, it tells us we need sleep. When it gets hungry, it tells us we need food. And our bodily felt experience of the world can tell us much more than basic physiological need if we listen to it carefully. In the cells of the body, in the coiled strands of DNA, in the photons that emanate from microscopic molecules, there is an inherited world of information that wants to be un-raveled and carried forth into the world.[3] This information provides each of us with a personal measure of our highest po-tential. It is what Emerson calls "the aboriginal Self, on which a universal reliance may be grounded, . . . it is that source, at once the essence of genius, of virtue, and of life. . ." (Emerson, 1984, p. 187).

As our personal inheritance, this information is much older than each of us and even those of us who are most keenly at-tuned to it will never fully realize or exhaust its depth and complexity. When we begin to attune ourselves to it, we real-ize that we are in the world and moved by the world on a level of intimacy that we cannot comprehend rationally. It is too close. We can only feel it. When we feel it deeply, we are moved by it. When we are carefully attuned to it, it gives us a power unlike anything we can know in the realm of the ego. "Here is the fountain of action and of thought," Emerson writes. "Here are the lungs of that inspiration which giveth man wisdom and cannot be denied without impiety and athe-ism. We lie in the lap of immense intelligence which makes us receivers of its truth and organs of its activity" (Emerson, 1984, p. 187).

The higher self is primarily a *receiver* of intelligence. It lis-tens for the source of immense intelligence that inspires all ge-nius. These ideas of genius are the firm, though elusive, un-derpinnings of our personalities that are carried forth into the world to the extent that our thoughts and actions are true to them. The inherited information and potential of the higher self changes and evolves much more slowly than the particulars of our historical circumstances. It is persistent and yet, so often the idle chatter and small concerns of the ego in the everyday world smother it. Faith in self gains strength by silencing the chatter of the ego and allowing the deeper personality to be unfolded and carried forth into the world.

The higher self, then, is the site of genius, the wellspring of the great ideas that move us to act in ways that are most true to who we want and need to be. It is this power to move us that most clearly distinguishes the ideas of the higher self from the concepts of the ego. The ideas of the higher self redirect our lives. When we are moved by an idea from the higher self, many, if not all aspects of our lives are reoriented and recontextualized around the force of that idea. Parents who are attuned to these ideas participate fully in the community; in fact they are often the beacons of community life. But they do not make fitting in a top priority. Regardless of what others may say or think, they are not afraid to bring a jug of water instead of donuts to an athletic event if they believe it is better for the children.

When we listen to the ideas of the higher self, they initiate in us a state of ultimate concern (Tillich, 1952, p. 3). Our ultimate concern as parents is related to guiding our children toward a healthy and self-sufficient adult life. The ideas we need to inform our task are often the same ideas that are carried around by the ego-self, but as such they fail to move us to action. They do not have the force to become principles for living. While contained within the ego, they are not of ultimate concern. Their power to move us is lost in the insecurities of the ego, which must contain them out of fear of losing its place in the sun.

I see this occurring frequently among college students, for example, who think about a career they would love to pursue or parents who dream about activities or tasks they want to try as something for others to do. Those lacking faith in their ideas see their ideal career as a far off fantasy. For some, the same idea that for so long fails to move them, at some point, often suddenly, becomes their own idea. The idea housed in the ego is suddenly attuned to the deeper, higher self. When it gains such attunement, one's entire life takes on new meaning. Courses in which students had no prior interest suddenly become eye-opening events because they see them as a part of the process that is leading to realizing the goal of the higher self. Their lives become reoriented around the pursuit of an idea, the same idea that a day or a week earlier had little effect on them.

When we pay attention to these ideas we realize that we do not generate them. Instead, we listen to them and learn to have faith in them so that we can identify with them. When we identify ourselves with such ideas, we enter into a state of ultimate concern. In a state of ultimate concern, our lives take on a purpose and a center, which serves to integrate all areas of our lives.

The power of these ideas can be formidable, like an adrenaline rush. But while the initial burst of energy that accompanies a great idea is necessary if one is to reorient one's life, it is not sustainable. For instance, a young college student may be moved by the idea that she wants to be a medical doctor. The idea has a powerful effect on her. She reorients her schedule in school to begin the process of getting to medical school. By the time organic chemistry comes around, the initial burst of energy is long gone. If the idea is to be realized, it must be transformed into principles for living, principles that will carry her through the difficult patches. Similarly, a parent might be moved by the idea that she wants to become an expert on healthy home cooking. The idea leads her to look at recipes, stock her cabinet with ingredients, and make some meals. In order for such practice to be sustained against the resistance of children and the temptation of ordering food in or eating out, however, it must become a set of principles for living.

To transform ideas into principles and to sustain them requires resolve, to be sure. But beneath this resolve, principles to live by are first adopted on faith because one doesn't know ahead of time if she can realize her dream or even if her dream is right for her until she tries to realize it. One will transform the initial idea and its energy into principles for living only if one has faith in the content of the idea, in her genius. One must believe in a medical career or healthy home cooking as a way of life if she is to sustain the arduous journey to realizing the idea. It is this belief, this faith, that will enable her to live a life of principle. And, according to Emerson, a life lived in accordance with sound principles is the only way that one can achieve peace with one's self and with the world.

In contrast, we know when we are not attuned to the higher self, when we are not at peace, when there is a dissonance within. This dissonance is felt when the ego-self is not moved by, and identified with, the powerful ideas of the higher self. This often occurs when the ego-self deceives itself into thinking that it can generate and control the ideas it needs. It fails to listen for the powerful ideas of the higher self, the ideas that come from beyond the confines of the ego. The ego is threatened by these ideas because they call the life and legitimacy of the ego into question, especially an ego that has been out of touch with the higher self. Under these circumstances, one experiences inner dissonance rather than inner peace and strength. This inner dissonance is a symptom of a loss of faith in the ideas of the higher self. This is the dissonance that results when we listen to the chatter of voices in the realm of the ego instead of the strong sure voice of the higher self. It is the lure of convenience that drives the family to the restaurant or the college graduate into a career that promises monetary reward with minimal sacrifice without regard for personal fulfillment. Convenience and short-term rewards keep those without faith in themselves, faith in their genius, from using their lives to realize their best ideas.

For parents, faith in the ideas of the higher self is critical. While the self does not generate these ideas exclusively, they are unique to the self. No two people will transform a great idea into principles and live in accordance with those principles in the same way. It is this uniqueness that requires faith because it is this uniqueness that moves a parent beyond social conventions and the comforting support that goes with them. To be unique requires faith because a great idea is a different idea. It is an idea that others do not have, at least not in the same way. Therefore, others will not immediately understand its relevance or its brilliance. It doesn't fit into their view of the world, which is why Emerson makes good sense when he writes, "To be great is to be misunderstood" (Emerson, 1984, p.

183). A person who is misunderstood by others needs faith in self. The first parent to show up to her child's soccer game with a jug of water for snack needs to have faith in herself, in her ideas, if she is to withstand the curious looks and whispers of parents and the moans of children who are accustomed to getting junk food. It takes faith in one's self to explain to a child that he can't have a video game that all of his friends have because it is bad for the development of his mind and reduces healthy physical activity. While we need not aspire to the astounding faith of Abraham, parents do need faith and resolve to shop, prepare, serve, and clean up a family dinner when take-out is available. But we need faith in our ideas if we are to live a life of principle and find peace. Once we uncover faith in ourselves, we can also find faith in the world, in particular, the world of the child.

Notes

1. For an illuminating discussion of the relationship between ethics and religious faith in Kierkegaard, see *Fear and Trembling*. For an excellent commentary on Kierkegaard, see *Transcendence and Self-Transcendence* by Merold Westphal. For a more challenging and provocative discussion of Kierkegaard's meditations on faith from a Derridian deconstruction point of view, see *The Prayers and Tears of Jacques Derrida: Religion without Religion*, by John Caputo.

2. I use the term genius here in anticipation of a discussion of Emerson's notion of genius in his essay "Self-Reliance."

3. In *The Field: The Quest for the Secret Force of the Universe*, Lynne McTaggart documents the scientific version of what Emerson is referring to as the divine inspiration of the aboriginal self.

CHAPTER TWO

FAITH IN THE WORLD

The second dimension of philosophical faith is faith in the world. Just as faith in the self calls for us to move beyond the ego-self, faith in the world leads us to perceive and interact with the world on levels that are not immediately apparent to everyday perception. The search for coherence, unity, or meaning beneath the constant changes that we encounter in the everyday world has been an integral part of the philosopher's journey from the beginning. By reflecting on the world of change, whether in nature, human nature, or society, philosophers seek deeper meaning and higher fulfillment than the nonreflective life can offer. Throughout history, philosophers have relied on reason to carry out this search. Reason seeks out and articulates order and meaning in an otherwise chaotic world.

Because of the power of reason to find and impose order on the world, the modern world offers us amenities that could hardly be imagined a generation ago. But this power is so alluring, we often overlook the fact that reason is not our primary access to the world. Upon close examination we find that reason stands on the shoulders of faith to conduct its business. Without faith in the world, faith that there is an intelligible order to the world and that it is worth getting to know the hidden order and meanings of the world, reason would not have the persistence and endurance it requires to achieve the success that it has. The philosopher's search then, while executed by reason, is fueled by a faith that beneath the apparent chaos and flux of everyday life the world has something that is knowable and worth knowing.

Philosophers who have carried out this search, however, warn of the difficulties it entails. It is a search that only a minority of people are interested in making. And the search can leave one feeling disoriented and isolated as well as a little insecure from time to time.[1]

Most parents are familiar with the feelings of isolation, disorientation, and insecurity. The task of raising children doesn't come with a how-to manual and often feels thankless as we move from one crisis to the next never quite knowing if we are doing or saying the right thing. The insecurity of not knowing often leads parents to follow the crowd, to do what others do, sign their children up for the popular activities and buy the trendy toys and clothes. From the prerational and insatiable desires of children to the irrational and defiant decisions and attitudes of teenagers, parents are constantly challenged to find coherence amid persistent and unpredictable change. And like the philosopher who knows that the search for meaning and truth is never complete, but a series of constant revisions, parents quickly realize that whatever coherence we may arrive at today will likely need to be revised tomorrow.

For both parents and philosophers, the challenge to find coherence is formidable. The point of this chapter is that parents share a motivational force with the philosopher that can strengthen the resolve of their search. This motivation is faith in the world. Without this faith in the coherence and meaning of the world, inquiry ceases and we are left to the wild winds of fortune to find our way from place to place and situation to situation. Philosophers have shown us that we can do better than conform to prevailing trends and that it is an inte-

gral part of a fulfilling human life to do so. Faced with the incessant demands and responsibilities of guiding children and responding to their needs, parents can and, indeed, must cultivate the same faith in the world that philosophical inquiry has relied on for centuries.

The World for Faith

The two most pervasive and enduring ways that we experience the world is through nature and through society. These two dimensions of the world encompass the most significant variables that shape our lives as individuals and as a species. For instance, the world as nature includes not only the natural environment of trees, rivers, drought, and famine, but also our genetic inheritance that defines the personal parameters we rely on to experience and respond to the world. The world as society includes social structures that range from the international to the local and includes economic, political, educational, and family influences. While no single work could adequately address each or any of these variables that constitute the world for us, there is ample evidence to show that they are all undergoing rapid change. Recent events remind us that some of these changes can be overwhelming. One wave in the Indian Ocean and a hurricane in the Gulf of Mexico destroy entire villages and cities while overpopulation, diminishing resources, and religious and political warfare threaten the social fabric of nations. In the United States, judges are gunned down in their courtrooms and homes while research commissions study the causes of rapidly increasing rates of depression in children and teenagers along with its devastating symptoms such as obesity, drug abuse, and suicide. These high profile events combined with the challenges we all face in family life generate uncertainty about the meaning and coherence of the world and our place in it.

For parents these uncertainties are magnified as they are concerned not only for themselves but for their children's future. There is good reason for their heightened concern as violence increases around the world along with the cost and competition for a good education. The economic future is also becoming more uncertain as the workforce becomes more global and more mobile, while scientists make dire predictions about the health of our environment. And for parents of children with special needs, there are more immediate concerns than the competition for a place in college. They must search for adequate health care and struggle to create an environment in which their children's needs are met. These are challenges that require immense courage, perseverance, and beneath both of them, faith.

Unfortunately, the lack of direction and insight that many professional, political, and business leaders often demonstrate regarding these issues can often leave parents feeling alone and vulnerable, if not helpless. These feelings can add to the anxiety of parents as they contemplate their children's future. But as Plato's parable of the sea navigator reminds us, we shouldn't always expect those in power or the declared "experts" to be the best leaders. In chapter 1 we saw the need for faith in self. Faith in self needs to be supplemented with a faith in the world if we are to sustain our difficult task of finding some order and meaning in the midst of chaos, destruction, and the shallow perspectives of popular culture. With the appropriate faith, the world as nature and the world as society can be transformed from a source of anxiety for parents to a source of strength that will assist them in meeting the unique challenges of parenting today.

Faith in the Natural Order

Thomas is twelve years old. He is quiet and reserved. He likes to keep to himself. He is also very creative and bright. He participates in theater and is always at the very top of his class in school. Since he is quiet and he does not have many friends, it was difficult for his parents to know how he was feeling about his new school. They were delighted when he was picked for the cast of a play in the local theater group. He was animated about participating and began socializing with his fellow cast members. His adjustment to the new school seemed to be well in hand and they were relieved. But if you're a parent, you know there is always a new source of anxiety around the corner. A week after the play had finished and Thomas's mother dropped him off at school. Thomas left the car as happy as she had seen him. When she picked him up, he waited until he got into the car and began to cry.

A group of girls began to taunt Thomas saying that he was gay because of the way he walked. Thomas tried to ignore them, but they were relentless and had a long laugh at Thomas's expense. His mother was devastated. She felt his hurt more deeply than Thomas did. That evening Thomas's father came home and heard the story. He is not quiet, shy, or small. He also felt Thomas's pain, but he didn't want Thomas to see that. He was going to be decisive in order to teach Thomas to be decisive. Thomas's mother thought that they should contact the counselors. Thomas begged them not to. His father agreed that it was not the best way to handle the problem. He knew that Thomas had to confront the girls if he wanted the taunting to stop. He told Thomas this and he told him what he needed to say. This was difficult for Thomas because confronting them and saying what his father prescribed was out of character for him. But his father insisted that he practice by making Thomas say it to him. He gave him a couple of options depending on how the girls would react to his initial comments. Thomas practiced until he got comfortable in his role. The next day the girls started as they had the day before, looking at Thomas with a giddy menace. With butterflies in his stomach, Thomas turned and walked straight toward them. He told them that he did not know them, they did not know him. He had no problems with them and did not know why they had a problem with him. He also told them that he would prefer if they could continue without problems, but if they continued to laugh at him, they would regret it. This was all said in the vernacular that Thomas's father had taught him the night before and could not be repeated in the presence of any school counselor or teacher. It was out of character for Thomas to speak profanities but the strategy worked. The girls realized they picked on the wrong kid and Thomas realized that had just put their disrespectful behavior in its place. And he felt really good about that. In fact, he felt great.

Many of those who comment on parenting and child development might disagree with such a confrontational approach. While I might not have offered the same advice, I admire Thomas's father for the faith he had in himself and in his son. I also admire Thomas for turning into the problem rather than trying to avoid it. His father taught him not to turn away from the injustice, the meanness, the chaotic behavior, but to confront it. His father had faith that by confronting the problem, the best resolution would be found. This couldn't be known ahead of time. It could only be discovered by turning toward it, by confronting the problem. Thomas's father demonstrated the faith that drives the philosopher's inquiry.

Since the first philosophers, the pursuit of knowledge and wisdom has been driven, in part, by the belief that the world is knowable. The pre-Socratic philosophers relied very heavily on faith in the world as they sought out a unifying principle that held together and guided the impermanent flux of the changing world. As we do today, they observed things coming into being and passing away. What distinguished them as the first philosophers is that they looked beneath the surface of these processes for the unifying laws or principles that were guiding them. In this regard, perhaps the most noteworthy of the pre-Socratic thinkers was Heraclitus who scorned those who failed to see the *Logos* that was beneath their noses. In his philosophical fragments, Heraclitus used concrete images such as fire and rivers to point to the intermingling of the one and the many, unity and diversity, coexisting in the same event or phenomenon. One cannot step into the same river twice he told us because it is always changing. But it is not just rivers or the flames of fire that change; the world, and all that constitutes it, is in constant flux (McKirahan, 1994). In the morning a boy goes to school happy and returns in tears.

By emphasizing the constant flux that we encounter and live with in the world, Heraclitus reminds us of the powerful tendency we have to search for permanence, security, and comfort. We often desire to escape or withdraw from the flux and impermanence of life. We long for a retreat from the tensions and demands placed on us by children, by work, and by the world in general. Many of us line up for lottery tickets and dream of a life of contentment in which we do not have to prepare food that children won't eat, worry about mortgages, or feel the anxiety of a looming deadline. But such a life is fantasy. It is self-deception and it distracts us from devoting our full attention and energy to the actual events at hand in the world. Heraclitus was very direct in expressing his disapproval of such a life, comparing it to the life of cattle or dogs "who bark at everyone they do not know" (McKirahan, 1994). Heraclitus's thought encourages the opposite of escape. To him, there is no need to escape from the world if we understand it properly. Rather than escaping, Heraclitus turns toward the world and its strife to find meaning, to find coherence, to find the *Logos*. This turning-in is unsettling initially because we come face to face with the everlasting impermanence of things and the uncertainty and unpredictability that goes with it.

But Heraclitus can face the strife that constitutes the world because he has faith in the world. He has faith that by turning toward the world, by inquiring and searching for the *Logos*, the coherence and meaning that lie hidden in nature, he will be rewarded with a better life. Instead of being tossed and turned by the perpetual changes that the world constantly throws at us, he sees the calm within the storm. But to see this calm, one must be calm. And seeing the calmness in the world reinforces the calm that is required to see it. This way of seeing and experiencing the world can never be found by escaping from the flux, or by merely attending to the surface appearances of the changing world. This search requires that we acknowledge, accept, and face up to the impermanence and unpleasantness of things. Sometimes we must tell our child to confront the bully. It can be uncomfortable and disorienting, which makes it tempting to join the crowd, give in to the latest trend, or escape into diversions.

This search is particularly uncomfortable for parents who have achieved the means to acquire the comforts of contemporary life. We do not have to look far, however, to realize that acquiring such comforts does not shield us from the difficulties and dangers of raising children. Dangerous and unacceptable behavior is found in all sectors of society, rich and poor. Hence it was sad, but not surprising, when I recently heard of an upper-middle-class seventeen-year-old boy convincing a twelve-year-old girl to perform oral sex on him while he recorded her in the act and placed it on the Internet for his friends to see. These children have all the trimmings of a comfortable life, but their actions reveal a disturbing lack of respect on the part of the boy and a dangerous lack of judgment and self-esteem on the part of the girl. For the parents of these children, there are difficult questions to be asked of their children and of themselves. What would lead someone to treat a young girl with such hostility? Where did this young man get the idea that such behavior is acceptable? What would lead a girl to feel like she should capitulate to a young man's twisted appetites? Why was a twelve-year-old allowed to be in such a situation?

In the short term it is easier for parents in situations such as these to blame the other or to rationalize the behavior, convince themselves that it is an aberration and not a part of a deeper pattern. The adult mind has many tools for escaping the difficulties of parenting. And escaping the difficulty is always tempting. But a parent's faith in the world will enable her to resist this temptation. And in doing so, she will demonstrate the virtues of courage, strength, and faith: the faith that there is more to the world than we know. These virtues make it possible for us to see beyond the unpleasantness, chaos, and impermanence. Using philosophers as our guide, we can hope that over time, these virtues not only help us to get through each day, but that they can contribute to a much more satisfying life.

Commenting on Heraclitus, Nietzsche (1998) explains this dynamic in the following way.

> The everlasting and exclusive coming-to-be, the impermanence of everything actual, which constantly acts and comes-to-be but never is, as Heraclitus teaches it, is a terrible, paralyzing thought. Its impact on men can most nearly be likened to the sensation during an earthquake when one loses one's familiar confidence in a firmly grounded earth. It takes astonishing strength to transform this reaction into its opposite, into sublimity and the feeling of blessed astonishment.

Sublimity and blessed astonishment are feelings that await the one who has faith, along with strength and courage, to wade in the midst of the changing tide rather than scramble for shore. The longing to avoid unpleasantness and impermanence and the longing for contentment, security, and predictability often prevents us from finding the deepest meaning and the highest rewards that can be found by inquiring into nature and the impermanent and changing world.

Heraclitus was at home in the world because his inquiries were sustained by a belief that the world is ordered and therefore knowable. This belief led him to become familiar with the divine, which for him was also in the world, not outside the world. His perceptual gaze found the divine dwelling amidst the apparent chaos. He taught us that human consciousness has access to the divine through the proper use of reason. Reason gives us the capacity to understand the laws and patterns that govern the way the world works and the way things come into being. Heraclitus saw these patterns and laws, these unifying principles, the *Logos*, as expressions of the divine presence in the world. So even though Heraclitus is not a theologian, he saw human experience finding its deepest meaning by recognizing the presence of the divine in the world. This recognition is achieved by using reason to understand the order beneath the changing world.

Parents have an opportunity to achieve this same recognition in their children. The fullness of life, of divine presence, is what we experience in loving our children unconditionally, when we step back from the intensity of everyday life to appreciate the incomprehensible beauty and mystery each child conveys in the world. Parents empty themselves in loving their children. In doing so, they make room for receiving the fullness of meaning and (divine) presence in the world. Most of us, however, rarely have time for such appreciation. In meeting the demands of everyday life, we rely on faith that it is there. And that faith motivates us to search for meaning and coherence in the midst of chaos.

It is in this search for order that Heraclitus, religious thinkers, and parents have a lot in common. For instance, we all agree that the world is ordered and not mere chaos. Religious faith is grounded in the belief that God created and sustains the world with a plan and a purpose. Like the philosopher, responsible people of religious faith use reason to seek out order in the world. They accept that the world is knowable, but only to a point. Those who have faith in God as the creator point out that there is an unbridgeable gap between what the finite human mind can know and what God has in mind. Reason is to be used and trusted, but since it is finite, it must also accept that God's mind and intentions are beyond its capacities for understanding. When we reach the limits of rational understanding, we must depend on God's intervention, God's grace, for our highest fulfillment, for salvation. In Abraham we saw a faith in God's omniscience. In Abraham's mind, God knows what is best for him, even though God called for what seemed to be the worst for him. Abraham's faith in God is not just faith in the world, but also faith in a supernatural, suprarational world. Abraham may not have known why he was called to sacrifice his son, but he believed that the call was correct.

We have seen why Abraham's faith is extraordinary. It forced him to transcend the world of reason and justification and denied him the ability to receive support from reason or from reasonable friends. And while he was certainly alone and in a very unfamiliar place when he approached Mount Moriah, he was buoyed by a powerful conviction. Abraham's conviction that God knows what is best allows him to overcome the disorientation that the philosopher or the parent often feels in searching for meaning or coherence. Abraham is faced with the absurd, but his faith in God, in the supernatural, enables him to overcome his fear and trembling.

The faith of the philosopher and the parent is less dramatic, less courageous, even though it does go beyond what is known and what can be rationally justified. Because it is less demanding, it is more useful to parents. Like the faith of the philosopher, the parent seeks to go beneath the surface of what is readily apparent to everyday awareness. It searches for what is hidden and elusive. But unlike the faith of Abraham, the elusiveness of the insight and knowledge that the philosopher pursues is not a call to abandon reason entirely. It is a challenge that forces the thinking parent to extend the scope and capacity of reason to fortify opinions and justify theories, beliefs, and speculations about the way things are. The goal is always to search for a reasonable justification of the speculations and intuitions that we rely on in trying to understand and make our way through the world.

Unfortunately, some of those who are engaged in the pursuit of rational justification see it as an attempt to eliminate the elusiveness of the invisible, to reveal everything that is hidden to the rational mind. Those who see the pursuit as a means of overcoming and eliminating mystery fail to recognize the futility of such a task. Even though reason is powerful and the capacities of technology grow exponentially, there is always something hidden from view. As soon as we discover something new or achieve some clarity, we see something else in the shadows, unclear and unknown. As powerful as reason is, it misses the deepest source of meaning in human existence when it attempts to eliminate mystery and unpredictability from our experience of the world. So rather than trying to eliminate the mystery and elusiveness of the world, and more than just tolerating it, faith in the world enables us to appreciate mystery in a way that empowers us.

Parents have firsthand knowledge of the indelible nature of the unknowable, unpredictable, and mysterious. Any parent who has tried to understand or, worse, control the thoughts and behavior of children knows that it is a futile and frustrating task. We need to be reasonable with children, to be sure, but the parent–child relationship cannot be contained or explained by the reasonable alone. At the heart of these relationships are unspoken, often misunderstood, yet deeply significant moods, thoughts, and emotions. Although this unspoken and hidden world is not fully accessible to reason, it is full of meaning. In fact, it provides the context or background against which reason can meaningfully function. It provides reason with more than it can think about or know. The second dimension of parental faith is a faith in the meaning and the strength that comes from an awareness and acceptance of an ever-evolving, fluid, and incomplete understanding of this hidden, elusive, and often mysterious world. This philosophical faith echoes the faith of Abraham in that it places a trust in what cannot be fully known. And yet, it differs from Abraham's faith because the philosophical mind is always trying to support this belief and to understand with evidence and reason. It doesn't stop inquiring to pray for salvation. It does everything it can to find deeper knowledge and meaning in the world. So while philosophical faith does ask parents to go beyond the realm of what is socially comfortable and acceptable, it does not require that they abandon reason to leap into the abyss of the unknown with fear and trembling as Abraham did before God. Instead, the second dimension of philosophical faith can provide parents with strength and hope that is not available as long as we only perceive or impose arbitrary and whimsical structures and order onto the surface of everyday life, or worse, give in to the disorder and chaos that dominate the stories of our time. Faith in the world supports and motivates the search for meaning and coherence even in the midst of chaos.

The Erosion of Faith in the World

Unfortunately, there are signs that the second dimension of parental faith is eroding. Many will argue that the loss of faith in the world as society is inevitable because there are overwhelming social trends that cause it. For instance, some point to the increasing demand for two-income families as an acid that is burning away the fabric of family life. The price of housing, education, healthcare—the basics—has escalated to such an extent that it is impossible for most families to live on one salary. When both parents are out of the home, there is an immense impact on the family (see Warren and Tyagi, 2003). With less parental presence and intervention, children and adolescents are more prone to make poor decisions.

But it is not just the time away from the home that affects families and children negatively. In fact, Ellen Galinsky's research reveals that the biggest impact of these structural shifts on the social fabric of families is not that there is less time with the children (Galinsky, 2000). The bigger issue, as seen from the perspective of children, is that there is more stress in the home. Galinsky's studies show that children can cope quite well with time away from their parents if there is not excessive stress. A major reason there is more stress is that even with both parents working, they are finding it difficult to get ahead.

The two-income formula, instead of relieving financial burdens, has had the opposite effect. It has become a trap. As Warren and Tyagi (2003) argue in *The Two-Income Trap*, because there are so many parents competing for the same things such as housing and education in a safe community, the prices of houses have skyrocketed to absorb the second income. Desperate to get their children into good schools, parents bid against each other and end up pouring their disposable income into mortgages for houses in good school districts. But the spending does not stop there. There are food and clothing to be bought, activities, camps, and lessons to be paid for. After a while, many find themselves borrowing against equity in their home or against their paper income and putting themselves into debt. This leads to stress, which combined with the lack of time with children, creates the conditions for volatile relationships in the family. Children often become the outlet for a parent's frayed nerves. And even in the calm moments a working parent can feel strong feelings of guilt or even sadness for missing important moments in her child's development. These feelings are often followed by a desire to compensate.

Parents want to create the conditions in which children can be happy but their options for playing a positive role in that process are severely limited when they are forced to be away from them and stressed out when they are with them. A parent's busy schedule can make her feel as though she has to help her children find happiness at an accelerated pace. Just as the lack of time leads us to replace home-cooked meals with take-out, lack of leisure time leads us to try nourishing the spirit of children and the family with take-out. That is, we try to bring happiness and joy into the family and the lives of children prepackaged in the form of toys, elaborate celebrations, and, when they are older, cars and trips. There just isn't enough time together in the home to allow healthy family activities such as cooking a meal together, planting a garden, or playing a game to percolate. In trying to compensate for the lack of time, we allow ourselves to be sucked into too many out-of-the-home activities, or worse, we try to bring joy in the form of presents and treats into the home. But the frenetic schedules that result from too many activities exacerbate the time problem.

There are no quick and easy solutions for the needs of children and family. And just as a body limited to fast-food will eventually show signs of poor nutrition, the health of the family, in particular, the health of children, will deteriorate without the proper spiritual nourishment. When this occurs, there is little room for joy and, often, insufficient resolve to meet the challenges of family life in a prudent way. As the bonds of a healthy family shrivel away, the world can be seen as an unfriendly and unreliable place. This can lead to a loss of hope and faith in the world. Such a loss of faith whittles away at the motivation and drive of parents to seek what is best for themselves and for children.

This loss of faith is one way of explaining what is happening when children are handed uniforms and thrown on a field to play softball with donuts waiting for them on the sidelines before they learn how to play the game. The adults want the children to enjoy the game. They know that getting a new uniform is exciting to children. They know the children like donuts. And they are sure that children feel special to be a part of a team. Unfortunately, they forget to teach the children what they are supposed to be doing as a part of the team. This forgetfulness is a symptom of a loss of faith in the game and the game is representative of the world. That is, parents no longer trust that the process of learning the game step by step will be enough fun for children. And so we give them the trimmings of the game (uniforms and treats) without the substance. We sugarcoat their activities (sometimes literally) so they are sure to get immediate enjoyment from it. But for those who are given the chance to learn the game properly, there is a much deeper enjoyment. Like the musician who must practice repetitively in order to master her music, an athlete must be repetitive to master the movements and skill of a game. Without repetition, there is no mastery, even of the basics. Without mastery, there is less depth. Without mastery, there is less enjoyment. For one who masters the skill of a game or a piece of music, there are subtleties that will forever elude the novice. These subtleties make the game or the music a completely different experience, a different world, for the child who is exposed to the proper skills and techniques. Discovering and working with the deep structure of these activities, of a game, a sport, or a piece of music, along with the movements and skills that are required to play them, will always be decisively more rewarding to children than uniforms and treats.

We need to remind ourselves that the enjoyment that comes from a sugar treat or a new uniform is unlike the enjoyment that comes from working at an activity or a skill, which is not immediate. It takes time and is often laden with frustration and setbacks. Hence, in order for one to experience the deep enjoyment that these activities hold in store for us, we must have faith. That is, until we have experienced the joy of making the perfect play or playing a piece of music the way we want it to sound, we must have faith that these activities hold the potential for such rewards. One cannot know ahead of time if such a reward is there. We must go through the process to find out; hence, the need for faith, especially at the start.

Some will discover along the way that sport, or music, or some other activity that they are exposed to is not enjoyable. But that discovery is a valuable lesson for a child to learn. It is an opportunity for a child to make a decision to leave something behind, even if her friends do not. It is an opportunity to let her parents know that she feels different than they do about an activity. That is, it is an opportunity for a child to discover, form, and express other parts of her emerging personality. By working through these activities she learns more of who she is and who she is not. This lesson is obscured and delayed, if not lost, when we sugarcoat the activities of children and shield them from the challenging processes of learning a skill properly. By making the games about uniforms and donuts, we are teaching them to be consumers rather than actors. We are teaching them pleasures that come from being passive, rather than pleasures that come from being active and creative. And children are going to need all of the support they can get to resist settling for passive pleasures as they mature into teenagers and adults in a society driven by marketing and consumption.

While the worlds of sport and music may be innocuous activities of childhood, they reveal emerging attitudes toward social structures and patterns. These same attitudes turn up when we apply an analysis of philosophical faith to more significant parental involvement in childhood activities. Approximately three years ago, when I was doing research for *The Whole Child*, it was estimated that six to eight million children in the United States were being prescribed a psychotropic drug such as Ritalin or Aderoll. That estimate is now up to twelve million. This is a disturbing trend that indicates a dramatic loss of philosophical faith. These drugs are used primarily to help students to concentrate for longer periods of time in school. But there are a couple of unwarranted assumptions at work in administering these drugs to children so freely. One, it is assumed that the educational structure that is in place is the best one for all children. Two, this practice assumes that if a child can't compete within the educational structures in place, they can't succeed in life. Those administering and advocating the use of these drugs are working with a very narrow definition of success that is modeled on a narrow vision of educational success. It fails to recognize the extraordinary diversity of a child's personality. This diversity, if handled with insight or just accepted with care, can result in character strengths that will emerge later in life. The excesses of a child's personality resemble the excesses of our world. The philosopher respects these excesses and continues to inquire and probe to better understand and cultivate them. Children are more likely to become comfortable with themselves as they mature if their parents, teachers, and all adults who deal with children become like the philosopher, who respects the excess of the (child's) world without fully understanding it. By medicating a child so that he will conform to a narrow educational protocol, we dilute, alter, and possibly eliminate potential character strengths that lurk latently in the elusive background of the child's personality. In order for a parent or educator to work toward developing alternative character strengths, she must have faith in what can emerge from working with the whole person, a faith in the diversity of human capacities. More broadly, we need faith in healthy social structures, including healthy family structures, working together with nature to build on the strengths of children and to overcome deficiencies in a child's ability to learn.

But what about more severe health issues that go beyond just lapses in concentration? How can a faith in nature and social structures help here? Some children are let down by nature and are forced to endure conditions for which we have no remedy. It is often the case that parents turn to religious faith precisely when they realize that science and medicine have no answer, no effective protocol, to make their child better. They recognize that the health that they want for their child requires an extraordinary intervention. So they ask God for help. They look beyond faith in nature and social structures, beyond philosophical faith for answers or at least support. In these cases, one has to wonder if there is a role for philosophical faith. If science and medicine can't help, if nature has let the child down, how or why should one have faith in nature or in the social institutions such as medicine that have been developed to work with or correct nature?

After the initial emotions of fear, anger, and sadness, a common feeling that parents experience is frustration because of the lack of understanding that pervades their world. This lack of understanding not only determines their relationship to the medical condition but also shapes their relationships with the child, each other, and the world. It can be overwhelming for a parent to realize that the best scientific minds have yet to find a corrective for their child's condition. This causes some to give up, to lose faith in reason, in nature, and in the world. In such cases the turn to religious faith is understandable and to be encouraged since it can provide stability and hope to families. And as some studies show, prayer can even aid in the recovery from illness.[2] But while a turn to religion can be helpful in many ways, it ought not preclude philosophical faith.

For some parents, an ailment that besets their child is a life-altering event. It becomes the focal point of the family and they seek to understand all there is to know about their child's condition. They seek advice for themselves about how to deal with their own feelings and with each other. The parents become experts in the area they must address and in doing so, they are best able to care for their child. In these cases, parents are driven by love but they also exhibit a powerful faith in the world as they dive into the literature and consult with the experts.

The parents who can do this are exceptional because they do not stop with the disappointing words that come from the experts. Where many parents, understandably, accept the treatments prescribed by the experts, even if the treatments are ineffective or potentially damaging, the exceptional parent plows ahead, searching, inquiring, and eliminating protocols that do not work, sometimes against the expert's advice. Driven by love and faith, even with no clear answers in sight, their search is intense. As they find better protocols, they courageously eliminate bad or ineffective advice and take heart in finding experts who think differently and devote their lives to finding treatments outside the mainstream institutions.

These parents exemplify philosophical faith on a number of levels. They clearly demonstrate a deep faith in themselves. They know when an expert's advice and prognosis is acceptable and when it is not. They know that if they ask the right questions to the right people they will be able to compare and contrast expert opinion. But they also demonstrate a deep faith in the world. The search for better modalities, the unwillingness to settle for what they find unacceptable, demonstrates a faith in both the natural order of things to shine through in a way that benefits the child, as well as a faith in bodies of knowledge and the formation of new knowledge to render better protocols to treat elusive and difficult conditions.

For many parents, searching through and eliminating medical treatments of conditions that mainstream medicine cannot adequately address lead them to alternative experts that have learned to work with nature. They recognize the body as a mode of nature and find the optimal alignment between the individual child and the forces of nature that will benefit the child the most. The primary rule of such experts is to do no harm to the patient. They search for the least invasive procedures and try to stimulate the body's natural defenses and natural drive to be healthy. They seek to overcome the body's ailments by compensating for its deficiencies. The impetus to work with nature is an example of a profound faith in nature, a faith that is supported by reason, research, and results. And these approaches to the most difficult situations also demonstrate a profound faith in the child to work through the ailments and conditions to enjoy life to her highest potential.

While extraordinary circumstances call for extraordinary parents, we all have something to learn from their example. Very often, the protocols followed by parents with special circumstances are advisable protocols for parents without special circumstances. When parents develop a diet that minimizes toxins in order to offset the effects of medication, I wonder why parents of children who are not taking medication are complacent in allowing toxins to take root in their children's diet. These parents recognize that it is not only easier to have their children follow a prescribed diet if they follow it, they also realize that it is good for them to follow. It is easy to become complacent as a parent, especially when we have access to an abundance of material goods. The faithful parent recognizes that complacency is dangerous to the well-being of parents and children alike. Faith in the world helps us to avoid complacency, as does faith in our children. It is this faith that gives us the strength to turn into the problem rather than avoid it. Just as Heraclitus turned into nature to find the *Logos*, Thomas's father taught him to turn into the problem to resolve it. Ultimately, a parent's faith in his child will play a large role in determining the degree to which the child will fulfill his potential. It is to this dimension of philosophical faith, faith in the child, that we will now turn to supplement our account of philosophical faith in the world.

Notes

1. See Books VI and VII of Plato's *Republic* for a classic account of the philosopher's isolation from society.

2. See chapter 11 of *The Field: The Quest for the Secret Force of the University* by Lynne McTaggart for a description of scientific studies that demonstrate the effectiveness of prayer on the healing process of patients.

CHAPTER THREE

FAITH IN THE CHILD

Children are worlds unto themselves. Since philosophical faith includes faith in the self and faith in the world, the philosophical faith of a parent also includes faith in the child. In each child we see a unique coalescence of nature and society. Through its genetic and cultural inheritance, each child receives the gift of a deeply rich and complex past. Just as the philosopher must look beneath the surface, beneath the flux of everyday life in order to discern the meaning and intelligibility the world has to offer, parents need to look beyond the surface of a child's life to appreciate and cultivate the vast depth and potential they carry into the world. This appreciation and cultivation requires faith in what we cannot fully comprehend or see in the life of the child.

As a world unto itself, there are dimensions of the child's world that remain hidden and mysterious, beyond the conceptual grasp and beyond the direct influence of parents. Just as any inquiry into the aspects of the world at large generates more questions along with more knowledge, the closer we examine and interact with children, the more we understand and the more questions we have. It is this excess of being, the mysterious and elusive dimensions of the child that leave room for faith. As Paul Tillich (1957, p. 16) points out, "faith is uncertain insofar as the infinite to which it is related is received by a finite being. The element of uncertainty cannot be removed, it must be accepted." Or as Kathleen Norris (1999, p. 169) puts it, faith is not "synonymous with certainty. . . . It is the decision to keep your eyes open."

The responsible philosopher knows from the start that the world, reality, or being is always in excess of our ability to know and understand. The pursuit of truth is never complete and this makes it possible and necessary for us to continue searching. But we continue because we have faith. We have faith that the inquiry into what we do not understand is worthwhile. Life is better when we inquire. But we also have faith in that which is beyond our comprehension. We accept and affirm that which remains hidden and eludes the concepts of reason. This is especially true when it comes to the world of children. The deep source of a child's potential, of his emotions, feelings, and allurements is always in excess of what we can know about it. In fact, that which we observe in a child's life, the visible, is but a trace of the infinite, the invisible, out of which each child emerges (Levinas, 1969, pp. 33–44).

Faith as an Ultimate Concern

Tillich (1957, p. 1) defines faith as "a state of being ultimately concerned." When something compels us to be ultimately concerned, Tillich argues, it also demands our total surrender. In the Old Testament, Abraham, the father of faith, demonstrates the total surrender of genuine religious faith. He put his life and his son's life in God's hands. In religious faith the relationship is between a finite and an infinite being. One places faith in God with the hope of achieving total fulfillment, which is impossible in the realm of the finite. Through religious faith, we retain the hope of transcending our finitude through the assistance of God.

While the scriptures are clear that religious faith demands total surrender to God, many find themselves lured into placing their faith, their ultimate concern, in things other than an infinite God. For many, the promise of complete fulfillment is often placed in wealth, or country, or pleasure. There are all too many examples of people who have made the pursuit of wealth the centering act of their lives. They surrender themselves to the pursuit believing that wealth will one day provide the fulfillment they seek. Others surrender themselves to a political movement or a life of pleasure seeking hoping to find their fulfillment there. Of course, we know the outcome of their misplaced faith. After each success there is the inevitable feeling of emptiness, meaninglessness, and sometimes even desperation. For some, these disappointments eventually lead to a change of course. They place their faith in something more substantial and the centering act of the personality becomes a healthier site of integration for all of their concerns. For some, the desperation provokes a downward spiral, as they try to fill the emptiness with more of what causes it.

For all of us, the act of faith is risky. We can never be sure that we are placing our faith in the right things. We surrender ourselves to something in the hope that we are working toward fulfillment but we do not know. Whether it is money or God, the end result is beyond our comprehension. So we dive in and commit ourselves to the pursuit of something of which we see only its shadows, the trace of something that is always around the corner or over the next hill. In order to have faith, therefore, one must also have courage. One must persevere in the pursuit knowing that the end result may end up in failure and disappointment. There is, perhaps, no greater risk than the risk one takes in placing his faith in something because the result of misplaced faith is a loss of meaning in one's life. One discovers that he has surrendered himself to something that is not worthwhile. In choosing our ultimate concern, we are taking on the ultimate risk which requires the ultimate courage (Levinas, 1969, p. 18).

But what about a parent's faith in her child? For many parents, children are their ultimate concern. Parents and families orient their lives around the needs and concerns of children. Days are spent supervising homework and shuffling children from soccer to dance to music. This attention to the needs and activities of children requires parents to sacrifice their own interests. They surrender themselves to the lives and well-being of their children. In the process, parents seek fulfillment, consciously or unconsciously, through their children. The enjoyment of their children directly affects their own enjoyment and they see the success of their children as a direct reflection of their own success. While these orientations of parents toward their children display some of the central characteristics of faith, they leave open the question as to whether it is misplaced, misguided, or idolatrous faith.

This is an open question because there is a double risk for parents when it comes to placing philosophical faith in their children. On the one hand, they are placing their faith in what cannot be known, controlled, or comprehended. If Emmanuel Levinas is correct in describing the face of the human other as the trace of the infinite, the child is a parent's most direct and profound access to the infinite. But as the trace of the infinite, the face simultaneously reveals and conceals. It gives us something to know in what it reveals to us. But the more we get to know what is revealed, the more we come to see the mystery hidden in the infinite from which it comes.

Insofar as children are both finite and a trace of the infinite, parents can, and indeed, must have faith in the infinite and mostly hidden dimension of a child's life. This is the dimension out of which the character, resiliency, and mettle of the child will be forged with the assistance of a parent's love, skill, and insight. In the hidden depths of the child's developing personality is the power to become that which we cannot fully anticipate. So parents are faced with the task of simultaneously nurturing and cultivating the seen and unseen dimensions of a child's personality. And these different dimensions are not clearly demarcated. They are interwoven with each other, the one affecting the other in multiple ways. As parents, we must focus on the visible, on what we can know, with full awareness that what we deal with in the visible realm affects, and is affected by, the background that we do not know and cannot see.

Tolerance, Hospitality, and Forgiveness

The incomprehensibility of the hidden dimensions of a child's life can be exasperating for parents. Often the most difficult situations for parents are those in which there is uncertainty and ambiguity. A child begins to whine, complain, and cry, sometimes for days at a time it seems, and for no obvious reason. The parent tries to soothe her, to understand what is bothering her, but sometimes there is no reasonable answer. The causes of her agitation are unclear to mother and child, making the situation difficult to address. As adolescents, children challenge parents with a full range of mysterious and incomprehensible behaviors from brooding in silence, refusing to communicate, to promiscuous sexual relations.

Faced with the difficulties and unpredictability of our children's emerging personalities, it sometimes seems as though even bad news is better than not knowing because it gives us a sense of direction, a point of reference from which we can formulate a strategy and orient our lives. When the hidden dimension of a child's life is beyond our comprehension and ambiguous, it can be paralyzing. A parent who is unable to decide, to act, to guide, to nurture, to discipline may begin to feel like a failure. Entrusted with the responsibility to do all of these things, and do them properly, parents are expected to have the appropriate information and strategies. It is as if children, and society at large, are giving parents the message that a sports apparel company uses in one of its advertisements, "impossible is nothing."

To think the impossible is nothing can be a motivational trick to encourage athletes to push their training beyond the ordinary. But the later writings of French philosopher Jacques Derrida inspire by taking the opposite approach. For him, the impossible is something. In fact, according to Derrida, we need the impossible. We work toward the impossible; we desire it, seek it, and chase it. But unlike the athlete who is seeking to conquer it, the philosopher is more realistic. He knows we can't catch it. It is its very nature to remain beyond our grasp. But even in its irreducible elusiveness and otherness, the impossible has a profound effect on us.

For Derrida, working toward the impossible means working for justice, for forgiveness, for hospitality, with the full awareness that their realization will be perpetually deferred. These impossible ideals, ironically, make human life bearable. They open the possibility of pursuing those ever-elusive goals that provide the deepest meaning to our lives. If all we ever aspired to could be achieved, the meaning of our lives would be swallowed up by the world of the familiar, the world of our own making, the world of what is all too possible. Our world doesn't allow for pure justice to reign, but without the ideal, injustice becomes acceptable. The abuse and murder of a child is impossible to forgive, but we entertain the hope for the impossible lest our spirit become permanently vengeful.

For Derrida, philosophical faith is a faith in the impossible.[1] It is an affirmation of that which we will never fully own, grasp, control, or even understand. It is a hope for what is to come, even if it never arrives. For parents, it is the perpetual hope that our children will be happy and fulfilled knowing that these human conditions are elusive, never complete, and require persistent effort and extraordinary insight. And beyond hope, a parent's faith in the child demands the repeated affirmations of her children along the way, even when they discourage and disappoint. This faith is the affirmation of what we don't see, of what they don't display, but what we long for and wish for them. It is demonstrated repeatedly in a parent's effort to teach what is valuable and to discipline what is unacceptable, even when we are exhausted, because we have faith that our children can learn principles and parameters that will be useful to their pursuit of a fulfilling life. It is this affirmation and this hope that pushes and enables the parent to see beyond what is apparent, reasonable, familiar, believable, or even possible.

So a parent is called to look beyond for what is not visible while simultaneously focusing on what is in front of her. The hurt bodies and feelings, the tears and tantrums need immediate care while the hidden forces of the child's behavior beckon for our attention, calling like a faint whistle in the shadows, "Hey, Mom, over here." But they're gone before she can look.

Effective parenting searches for the pivot, the center, a balance around which competing forces swing in and out of our awareness. Parallel to the task of keeping the visible and the invisible dimensions of a child's developing personality in focus is the task of being simultaneously tolerant and hospitable. Derrida distinguishes these two attitudes toward others by identifying tolerance as conditional hospitality (see Borradori, 2003). As conditional hospitality, tolerance is the attitude which says that you are welcome in my home as long as you abide by my customs and rules. Tolerance makes clear, and retains, the sovereignty of the stronger. In the case of families, it is the parent who is tolerant of the child since it is the parent that sets the rules and customs of the home.

At the same time, however, the child calls for hospitality, an unconditional welcome. The unconditional welcome offered to a child is born out of the primal love a parent has for her child. Beneath the terms and conditions that will be tolerated in the daily lives of any given home, we strive to offer a loving acceptance of the child, even when the incomprehensible dimensions of her personality lead to disappointment, frustration, and confusion. This hospitality provides the strength to continue teaching, guiding, caring, and advising, even when it seems like there is nobody listening. Unconditional hospitality rests on the faith that we are moving in the right direction even though we cannot see where we are going or where we are leading our children. It is this faith that provides the parent of a sick child with the motivation to continue searching for the best treatment when information and expertise are scarce. It is the faith that beneath the rebelliousness of a child, even one who performs oral sex in a train station for recording, that somehow she is absorbing lessons and habits for living that will emerge later and serve her well when she matures into adulthood.

The balance between tolerating a child on conditions that are imposed in order to guide, organize, and secure a workable home, and the unconditional hospitality that welcomes a child even when they are acting outside of the conditions of tolerance is difficult to find and maintain. Tolerance and unconditional hospitality fight for a parent's attention, as does conditional and unconditional forgiveness. The tension that mounts between conditional and unconditional forgiveness becomes clear in times of crisis and conflict. On the one hand, parents have a responsibility to check children, to reprimand and punish them in response to wrongful behavior. Conditional forgiveness is contingent on the punishment being served. A teenager's free time with friends after school might be denied until a room is cleaned, a toddler's rudeness to others will be forgiven only after time alone in his room, and funds to an alcoholic family member may be cut off until she seeks out the help she needs. These are difficult, sometimes gut-wrenching, decisions that parents must make. But without reasonable conditions that are steadfastly enforced, civility will escape family life.

But to persevere as an effective parent, capable of joy and wholesome love, which are essential to the healthy development of children, we need to remain open to unconditional forgiveness. As difficult as it sometimes is, on some level, we accept our children as they are, in their incomprehensible difference from us and from what we expect. As the New Testament teaches us, it is the prodigal son that is most welcome at the dinner table, the one over whom the biggest fuss is made. To his sibling, there is no valid explanation for this fuss. In fact, to him it seems unfair. But the father remains open to his return, a return that is welcomed without any terms or conditions.

Unconditional forgiveness and unconditional hospitality are acts of faith. They are offered without justification and without merit. In offering these gifts to children, parents assume the risk inherent in any act of faith. In offering unconditional love, hospitality, and forgiveness we relinquish control. We acknowledge that we are at the mercy of the hidden dimensions of our children's lives, which we do not fully comprehend. In remaining open to behaviors, attitudes, and decisions that go beyond or even conflict with our expectations, we risk condoning what ought to be reprimanded.

On the other hand, by trying to retain too much control, we risk stifling what needs to be left alone and free in a child's personality. Whether intervening with conditions and terms, or letting the child be, we are called to walk a fine line between the seen and unseen, the known and the unknowable, the conditional and the unconditional. And each time we choose one of the two, we risk our credibility and our effectiveness as parents. Yet, we must choose. And as Kierkegaard reminds us, the meaning of our lives will be determined, in large part, by the seriousness with which we approach these choices. The choices we make become the life we choose (Kierkegaard, 1983). For parents, the choices we make also become, in part, the life our children will lead. Most often, our choices are made with only a partial view of the situation, incomplete knowledge of the relevant data. We choose with intensity, but we choose also with faith: faith in our children and the incomprehensible potential and resilience that resides beneath their laughs and tears, successes and failures, joys and pains.

Parenting by Substitution

Increasingly, it seems that it is faith in the resilience of children to overcome hardships, to flourish in the face of difficult challenges that parents lack. When this faith is absent, parents want to substitute themselves for their children in order to shield them from the world and its difficulties. They try to represent them, putting their own skills and their own mettle into the fire in place of their children, unsure and doubtful of their children's mettle. Such advocacy and representation often stunts the growth of the child as he internalizes the parent's doubt of his abilities. Finding it hard to resist the assistance, children take a back seat while their parents dispute, challenge, and argue with school officials, coaches, or other parents. The prognosis for these children is predictably bad.

I recently witnessed the results of such a parent–child relationship. On his way home from work, a teacher came across a number of students leaving a classroom, some very upset and crying. One was calling for the security guards and another asked the teacher if he would come to the room and help. As he walked to the entrance of the room, he heard a student loudly yelling profanities in the direction of an elderly professor in the classroom. He recognized the student because he was in the most recent edition of the school newspaper for beating up another student on campus. The teacher stepped into the classroom and asked the student to stop using profane language. The student became enraged, jumped out of his seat and began punching and kicking the teacher. Fortunately, the teacher was capable of defending himself and suffered minimal physical harm.

Inquiries into the situation revealed that this student had a number of incidents during his time at the college. In each case, his father, a lawyer, fought the college on every disciplinary measure they sought to impose. In fact, after assaulting the teacher, the family filed a multimillion dollar lawsuit against the teacher and the college alleging that he intentionally caused psychological harm to the student. It was as though the student was his father's client and his primary and sole function was to defend his son. In the process of defending him as a lawyer, however, he was inadequate as a father. While he was arguing for and receiving leniency from the college for all of his prior incidents, he was overlooking the more important task of trying to understand why his son was so angry and acting violently.

It is more important to our children that they be understood than represented. This young man needed an audience to which he could articulate the turmoil of his inner life because it was consuming him with rage and rendering him incapable of appropriate social behavior. The result of the father's one-sided, overprotective approach to parenting culminated in his son assaulting a teacher just two months before he was scheduled to graduate. Instead of attending a graduation ceremony with his classmates, he was appearing in court, responding to criminal charges.

It is critically important, of course, that children know their parents will protect and defend them. This is a child's primary source of security in the world. Without a sense that parents are on their side, children are likely to feel insecure, alone, and vulnerable. On the other hand, as this incident demonstrates, to protect a child when he is wrong, without attempting to understand him, without reprimanding him, or without getting him the help he needs to adjust his behavior, is to abdicate one's responsibilities as a parent. Such protection may appear to be an example of unconditional forgiveness, which is an essential part of a healthy parent–child relationship. But to forgive one's child for inappropriate behavior, either conditionally or unconditionally, first requires an acknowledgment that the behavior was wrong. Without a parent's acknowledgment of wrongful behavior, there is no forgiveness because he sees nothing to forgive. There is only protection through representation and substitution. Unconditional forgiveness must exist in balance with conditional forgiveness, which involves reprimand, sacrifice, and/or retribution.

The unwillingness or inability of a parent to acknowledge his child's wrongs leads to the overprotection of children. These parental weaknesses emerge out of two related sources. The first is a lack of faith in the child. And the second is a lack of principles. The lack of faith is symptomatic of the culture in which today's children are raised. Over the past twenty years in the developed countries, especially in the United States, many children have grown up with unprecedented prosperity and privilege. Life-threatening diseases have been virtually eliminated. Information is instant. Goods are ordered online and delivered to our doorsteps. Prior to 9/11, there was little they had to worry about. The hardships of life that previous generations faced no longer exist. On the whole, this is a very good thing. Parents want what is best for their children. But what is best is not always a lack of difficulty and hardship. One of the most important functions of parenting is to help our children develop the resources and resiliency they need to be self-sufficient, fully functional adults. Just as the body gets stronger by facing resistance, the character of a child will get stronger and more resilient by meeting and overcoming the difficulties and hardship of life. We do not need to create artificial hardships. The world will offer plenty of them. A child's hardships can range from a parent's insistence that she clean her room or her dish, even when she is tired, to coping with the death of a relative. Parenting also means holding children accountable when they do things that are wrong.

In order to hold a child accountable, we must have faith in children, in the resilience of their character. This resilience lies latent in the hidden and unformed depths of their developing personalities. It develops out of the excesses of their personalities, out of the qualities and forces that have yet to be adequately integrated into their lives, qualities and forces that are beyond our comprehension. Behind the tears and disappointment, and, perhaps, the anger, the hidden dimension of a child's personality responds to the trauma and the hurt, and works to repair and to heal. The child learns from mistakes and develops from adversity when she faces up to them. In offering children conditional forgiveness, we recognize that as they grow, they need to be held increasingly accountable for their actions if they are to become self-reliant adults.

Of course, conditional forgiveness is more effective when it is offered in a relationship that also enjoys unconditional love and forgiveness. The most recent research confirms what philosophers and psychologists have been arguing for millennia: Children who are cared for and loved in a safe and nurturing environment from the first days of life will develop the character strengths they need to prosper later in life.[2] These strengths enable one to overcome stressful and traumatic events more easily than those who lack the nurturing care during infancy and early childhood. Children who are loved and feel safe in the world are likely to be more resilient.

Principles as a Supplement to Faith in Children

The parent that overprotects his child not only lacks faith in his child, he also lacks an adequate awareness of and commitment to principles. In order to retain a healthy perspective on our children, what they do and how they develop, we need to

refer to principles that exist outside of the intimacy and intensity of our relationships. For instance, we need to have a
sound sense of justice if we are to know if our child is being
treated fairly. And we need to be committed to acting on the
principle of justice if we want our child to learn the benefits
of such a virtue, even when it makes life more difficult. An
awareness of, and commitment to, principles such as truth
and justice, allows parents to see their child and their relationship with their child in a healthy perspective. By relying
on principles, not just a child's feelings, in order to act, decide, or understand, parents open their perspectives to other
points of view.

Virtues such as truth and justice are also principles that we
can internalize to become a part of our character. The truly just
person need not look beyond himself for points of reference.
He can look within. The virtuous person instinctually strives
for the virtuous outcome. In fact, for the truly virtuous parent,
virtue takes precedence over the short-term interests of the
child. The virtuous parent not only has faith in his child, he
has faith in his principles. The parent trusts that his child will
be better off for sacrificing short-term interests for the sake of
virtue. He teaches his child to defer gratification for the sake
of principles because he knows that learning to live a life of
principle is more valuable than any short-term gratification
that violates principles. I recently became aware of a virtuous
parent who demonstrates a profound faith in his children and
in his principles.

Separating Twins

Tom is the father of six children ranging in age from nineteen to ten. Two of his children are twin boys. Tom is the most highly respected baseball coach in the area and has been coaching teams for a number of years. As the new season approached, parents and children were expecting and looking forward to having Tom coach the twelve-year-old team, since his twin sons would be on the team. Prior to tryouts, parents who were involved with the team held an organizational meeting. At that meeting, Tom informed the group that he would not be coaching the team this year. The rest of the parents were surprised and disappointed. When they asked Tom for an explanation, he responded in his calm, sincere, and mild-mannered way that everything was fine but he needed a break from coaching for a while. The focus of the meeting shifted to finding a different coach. Tom participated, as he always did, with his full attention to the task at hand.

Weeks later, at a birthday party, I came upon a conversation in which Tom was the topic of conversation. The gist of the conversation was that Tom is a model of integrity. From what I knew about Tom, it seemed very plausible that he was a man of integrity, but I was curious as to why they were discussing Tom's integrity at the party. I probed a little and discovered that his reasons for not coaching the team were more complex than just needing a break.

Tom's twin sons are very different personalities. They have different strengths and weaknesses. One is his own harshest critic and tends to dwell on his mistakes and failures while the other confidently looks to the next opportunity to prove himself regardless of his last performance. Not surprisingly, the latter is a more accomplished baseball player at this point in his life. He would clearly be an asset to the twelve-year-old team that was to be picked. On the other hand, his brother was just about at the cutoff point or perhaps slightly below the standard of the team. It is common practice that both sons would be picked by the team if their father were one of the coaches, and for good reasons. First, a father could not be expected to leave one twin at home while he was off coaching his bother. Second, in this instance, the brother with lesser ability was just slightly below standard and could possibly develop to the standards of the others over the course of the season. To the vast majority of fathers, this would be an easy decision: coach the team and accept the players the selection committee chooses, anticipating that both sons would be chosen.

Tom didn't agree with this approach. He stepped down from coaching because he recognized that if he coached the team, the committee would have chosen both sons while only one belonged on the team. By removing himself as coach, he told the committee to choose the players that deserved to be on the team on the basis of merit. It was easy to see that Tom was a man of unusual integrity. And his actions were doing much more than contributing to a better twelve-year-old baseball team. Tom's action was an example of deep philosophical faith in his child.

On the surface, one could interpret Tom's act as a lack of faith in his son. Some would argue that he would have shown more faith in his child by giving him a chance to improve. By keeping him off the team, this line of thinking goes, he was demonstrating a lack of confidence in his son or at least in his ability to improve as a baseball player. But Tom saw his decision as an opportunity to address much more than his son's baseball skills. Tom was interacting with his son and the team through the lens of honesty and justice. He respected his son so much that he was unwilling to deceive him. He respected his colleagues and their sons so much that he was unwilling to allow his son to take a place on the team that another child deserved.

Tom's respect for his son and for his colleagues and their sons was based on his faith in his son. He knew that his son would be disappointed. He knew that his son would likely accompany him to games as a spectator while his brother and his friends were playing. But he also had faith in the resiliency of his son's character. He trusted that his son would get past that disappointment and when he did, he would be a much better person. He would know the value of honesty and truth and know that his father is honest with him. He would be able to trust his father's word. He would also know that when he was chosen for a team or a part in a play, his place will have been well deserved. This knowledge is infinitely more valuable to him than improving his baseball skills. This knowledge will enable him to be comfortable with himself throughout life. Wherever he is, whatever group he is a part of, he will know that it is where he belongs. And all along the way, he will know what his father really thinks about him. Tom's faith in his son freed him up to act on principles that go beyond the mere short-term advocacy of his child. This faith also allowed him to be truthful with his son and to be concerned with justice for all involved.

Tom's action clearly displays the first dimension of philosophical faith, faith in one's self. His decision to keep his son from being chosen as a member of the team goes against the growing tendency of parents to overprotect or overadvocate for their children. Many of the fathers I talk to about this story admit that they would not be able to leave their son off the team because they would not want to disappoint him. They point out that it must have been especially difficult knowing that the boy's twin brother would be on the team. Tom certainly was troubled by this concern, but he recognized that in addition to exposing his son to the principles of honesty and justice, he needed to protect his son from the consequences of dishonesty and injustice. For instance, even though his son never said it, Tom sensed that he was aware of the difference in ability between his twin brother and himself. Tom was almost certain that the coaches that were selecting the team were aware of the difference in talent levels between the brothers. Given Tom's awareness of these feelings, it was easier for him to take the action that he did because he didn't want his son to go through an entire season knowing, on some level, that he might not belong on the team. Tom was going to be truthful with his son even if, in the short term, it was hurtful to him. No parent can fully know the effect of leaving one of two twin brothers off a team, but Tom had faith in his son. He had faith that he would overcome his disappointment. He had faith that he would become a better person, if not a better baseball player.

But his faith was not only in his son. It couldn't be. Such a faith would be idolatrous because faith requires total surrender in the hope of complete fulfillment. It is misguided, unfair, and idolatrous for a parent to hope that his child will somehow provide complete fulfillment for him. Tom's faith in his son was supplemented by his faith in the virtues of honesty and justice. He recognized that it would be inappropriate to totally surrender himself to his son's wishes. Parents have the responsibility to see beyond the potential disappointment of their children. In doing so, they need to be an example of how to identify and live by sound moral principles. Parents need to demonstrate their own resiliency by taking on their own difficulties and hardships without being consumed by them. These feats are not possible if one surrenders to the life of his child.

The Double Register

To have faith in a child is to remain open to and repeatedly affirm the unknowable, the unpredictable, and the irrational. At the same time that we work at meeting our obligation to be reasonable, to set limits and conditions by which children can live and learn, we are also required to accept and affirm what is beyond the reasonable. When they reject our advice and deny our requests, we can disagree and sometimes have an obligation to admonish, but we carry on with our affirmation of their lives. We feel disappointment, even anger, when they refuse to hear sound advice, but we retain our hope and our faith in them and their future. We remain open to their points of view and try to learn from their decisions, as well as our own, because we know that we do not have all of the answers to the questions of our own lives, much less of theirs. We know that what motivates and drives them is often beyond our comprehension. We listen, watch, and interpret, searching for the sense and the meaning in what they do. In fulfilling our obligation to provide conditions and limits in order to help our children develop healthy habits for living, we remain open to the unpredictable and often irrational forces of their inner lives and their future without conditions. This openness is a parent's faith in the child. And this faith protects us and our relationships with our children from being reduced to contentious power struggles and disheartening disagreements. This faith provides us with the psychological space to step back from our disagreements with their actions, decisions, and motivations. This space makes it possible for us to find new and creative ways of helping them to find their own way, their own voice, and their own principles for living. It enables us to help them accept the hidden dimensions of their own lives and to have faith in themselves and in us.

Finding and preserving the balance between the conditional and the unconditional, the seen and the unseen, is an art form, which Aristotle reminds us is very difficult because there are an infinite number of ways to get it wrong, but only one way to get it right (Aristotle, 2002, Book VI). The right action or decision is rarely the obvious or the easy one. Faith, Tillich reminds us, involves risk and to take risks we need courage. The courage to take risks is tied to the hope that the risk is worthwhile. Jumping off a bridge with a bungee cord tied around one's waist is a risk, but for the thrill-seeker it is worth it. Investing money in an unproven venture is worth the risk to the capitalist. To believe in a God without any hard evidence of his existence is to risk the meaning of one's life. But the promise of fulfillment is worth it to the theist.

Philosophical faith also involves risk. The more the philosophical mind probes and inquires, the more it seeks clarity and understanding, the more mystery and elusiveness it uncovers. The mysterious and elusive dimensions of the world and of our children's lives is not to be ignored, nor is it to be conquered. Philosophical faith recognizes the importance of this dimension and its meaning for our lives. This faith recognizes its ineradicable mystery, but it also recognizes the value and virtue of seeking a deeper and clearer understanding of it. In seeking this understanding, philosophers and parents alike rely on the faculty of reason. But like the other dimensions, a philosophical orientation toward parenting and our children, reason by itself is inefficient and often ineffective. It too needs to be supplemented by faith. Faith in reason is the fourth dimension of philosophical faith to which we will now turn.

Notes

1. I am taking the liberty of substituting philosophical faith for deconstruction. A philosophical justification of this substitution is beyond the scope of this work.

2. See research and references in the Commission for Children at Risk (2003).

CHAPTER FOUR

FAITH IN REASON

Faith without reason is blind and often destructive. The most obvious example of faith without reason is religious extremism. This type of faith is incapable of understanding or tolerating other points of view. It is suspicious and fearful of reason and points to some of the outcomes of modern rationality as evidence that we should choose faith in God over rational inquiry and discourse. To religious extremists, reason is the tool of morally bankrupt lifestyles that seek to impose themselves on others and in the process abandon God's special relationship with human beings. Whether radical Muslims using terror to murder people or Christian fundamentalists blowing up abortion clinics, religious radicals see no possibility of negotiating acceptable solutions through rational discourse. Instead, they form a hardened intolerance for anyone who disagrees with their point of view. This intolerance often leads to the vilification of others and, in extreme cases, their violent elimination. The world is witnessing the effects of faith without reason in the terrorism of fanatics who murder those with whom they disagree.

Responsible theologians, on the other hand, recognize the need for faith and reason to work together. Hence the motto that accompanies St. Anselm's work, *"fides quaerens intellectu."* Faith in God gives one who believes an orientation, a way of looking at the world. With this basic orientation in place, the reasonable person of faith does his best to understand the world. But because reason is finite and God is infinite, the reasonable believer understands that he will never fully reveal, name, or know God. Used properly, reason helps the believer to understand the world better while also making room for prayer, reverence, and mystery. This faith is not extreme and does not lead to violence. A reasonable faith recognizes that one's point of view is always limited and, therefore, other points of view should be respected, not eliminated. The theological relationship between faith and reason is healthy and informative in trying to develop an account of philosophical faith for parents. It demonstrates that religious faith can work together with reason to understand the world as sacred while recognizing the holiness of individuals in the world.

Philosophical faith also requires faith and reason to work together. Philosophical faith, however, brings reason and faith together with a different point of emphasis. Instead of faith *and* reason, philosophical faith is constituted, in part, by faith *in* reason. While the theological orientation points to the limitations of reason, especially its inability to know God, philosophical faith focuses on the power of reason and what it can reveal to us, especially when it comes to a parent's ability to know herself, her child, the sacredness of both, and the sacredness of the world in which we live. Philosophical faith holds an optimistic vision of what reason can know. But just as faith without reason is destructive, too much faith in reason can also lead us astray.

In fact, many philosophers are guilty of overemphasizing reason and transforming or reducing our rational capacities to instrumentality. As a result, many see reason as a tool employed almost exclusively for problem solving and achieving our self-interested goals. Using reason in this way revealed its incredible power over nature that has been increased exponentially by technology. The power of reason became so intoxicating to many philosophers, they began to think that there was nothing human beings could not accomplish if we only learned to use reason the right way. This mindset prevailed among the most prominent thinkers of the seventeenth century and it unleashed the powers of modern science. There are two questionable assumptions at the heart of this mindset: One, human reason stands outside of and independent from the laws of nature, and two, we all have the ability to be reasonable when necessary and appropriate. By declaring reason free from the laws of nature, we put ourselves in a position to uncover and understand these laws in order to control and change nature for the well-being of humankind. This approach to understanding nature has led to innumerable benefits for human beings. We have made medical advances that have alleviated immense suffering and increased the human life span by decades. We have developed technologies that have eliminated torturous working conditions for many in the industrialized world. We have climate-controlled homes and cars, access to instant information, and many other luxuries that technology and science make possible.

Of course there are problems that come with all these advances. These problems range from climate change that is being accelerated by energy consumption and the emission of greenhouse gases to rising cancer rates due to the technological manipulation of food supplies. But there are other important consequences of envisioning human nature as something apart from nature as a whole. The picture of human nature as a detached faculty of reason existing outside of the laws of nature has made it extremely difficult, if not impossible, to adequately understand ourselves and our place in the world. To misunderstand our own nature and where we fit into the larger universe in which we live and on which we depend, makes it impossible to live well, to live in accordance with what we are meant to be. Not knowing our place in the world is akin to an athlete who misunderstands the game he is playing. If he arrives on the basketball court thinking he is supposed to be a baseball player, he will not perform very well. He will be playing by the wrong set of rules and his actions will accordingly be inappropriate and ineffective. Similarly, if we do not understand what we are and what we are supposed to be, we cannot realize our potential, what it is we should be doing to express and realize our human nature. Of course there are several respectable philosophical accounts of human nature and how we fit into the larger world. I am not claiming to have a definitive version of our place and our nature here. But I do see it as useful to begin thinking about our nature and how to realize it by considering the simple fact that, we are, in addition to being rational, natural beings. We are a part of nature. And we cannot adequately understand ourselves if we ignore or deny our place in the natural order.

As natural beings, much of what constitutes who we are is embedded in the natural order of things. Hence an adequate understanding of who we are and who we can become requires an understanding of our place in nature. This understanding is best achieved through the careful and appropriate use of reason. Rather than overemphasizing the instrumental function of reason that seeks to impose its own structures onto the natural order of things, as well as our social and individual lives, reason can be used to interpret the information that is made available to us though nature and society. In developing the interpretive function of reason, we can not only look at the natural order as it presents itself to us from the outside, we can also turn the interpretative capacities of reason onto our own lives, in particular our emotional lives. By regarding emotions as natural, we have a better chance of understanding them and, in turn, understanding ourselves as a part of the natural order. So we need to be rational, but we need to recognize that our capacity to reason is bound up with many other facets of our lives, which, in turn, are governed by the processes and laws of nature. That is, in order to understand ourselves adequately, we need to see ourselves as a part *of* nature rather than apart *from* nature.

That we are a part of nature is one of the seminal insights of seventeenth-century philosopher Baruch Spinoza. For Spinoza, everything that exists is a part of one substance, which he refers to as *God* or *Nature*. Things come into being and pass out of being in accordance with cause–effect relationships that are governed by the laws of nature. One of the goals of rational thinking is to know these laws and what follows from them. To know these laws is to know, in part, the laws of *God* or *Nature*, or the laws of reality itself. Because everything is a part of this one reality, anything, when understood in the right way, can reveal to us the way reality is. That is, as long as what we know is known with adequate ideas, it will provide some knowledge of *God* or *Nature*. As Spinoza writes in proposition 24, Part V of *The Ethics*, "The more we understand particular things, the more we understand God" (1982, p. 216). To understand things in the context of God, or nature, in their deepest context is to achieve the highest contentment of mind or blessedness.

Since knowing things properly is to know them in the context of God or Nature, an adequate understanding of our children requires seeing how we fit into and are sustained by the laws of God or Nature. The most stubborn impediment to achieving this understanding is human emotions. Emotions can have a powerful effect on our behavior. As long as we fail to adequately understand what causes our emotions and, in turn, our behavior, they hold us in bondage. We deceive ourselves into thinking that we are acting freely when in fact our emotions are dictating our actions. The driver who races after another driver who cuts in front of him in order to give him the finger thinks he is doing so freely. In reality, the emotion of anger is compelling him to chase the other driver. The problem is that the anger is not generated solely from the actions of the other driver. The other driver is merely the trigger for anger that is held in reserve. As long as we fail to understand the causes of our emotions and actions, we cannot realize our true potential and we cannot adequately guide our children toward healthy adulthood. On the other hand, by using reason to understand the causes of our actions and our place in God or Nature, we can attain the highest freedom and contentment of mind.

Spinoza's account of human nature, the power of reason, and the freedom and happiness that we are capable of achieving is intoxicating. Yet there is a critical element missing from his thought without which it is difficult to see how his account of the power of reason can be useful to nonphilosophers, including parents. In fact, one of the primary motivations for this book came from a colleague and parent who raised some tough questions in response to an article I wrote entitled, "Parenting and the Retrieval of Intuition." One of the points of this article was to show that Spinoza's account of reason can be very effective in the context of family life, in particular, in understanding emotions in parent–child relationships. My colleague could easily see the potential of reason to solve problems by understanding the causes of emotions, thereby diffusing their power over our behavior. What was less clear in the article, however, was how a parent summons the strength or discipline to actually be rational in the face of family chaos and crisis. How does a parent "turn on" reason when the overwhelming temptation is to respond instinctively and emotionally? What is it that makes a parent choose to be reasonable when a child pushes her buttons to make her angry? How do we maintain that composure in the midst of chaos and powerful emotions?

The answer to these questions lies in philosophical faith. That is, only if we have faith in ourselves, in the intelligibility of the world, and in reason's ability to know the world will we attempt to be reasonable in the face of the unreasonable. And so in this chapter, I want to show that along with faith in self, faith in the world, and faith in the child, *faith in reason*, as a component of philosophical faith, can contribute to effective parenting. In cultivating a healthy faith in reason, parents can find a balance that avoids the pitfalls of overemphasizing reason while also recognizing the power of being reasonable.

The Power of Reason

Philosophy is fundamentally a rational enterprise. Philosophy is the pursuit of wisdom and the vehicle of that pursuit is reason. Reason enables us to think clearly, to understand the world better, to recognize order where there is disorder, and to find meaning where there is confusion. Rational thinking enables us to plan ahead, anticipate the outcomes of our decisions and actions, and to avoid harmful behaviors and situations. Reason also allows us to step back from our immediate surroundings to consider a situation from another's points of view and make better informed decisions. For parents faced with the task of guiding children who are driven by the irrational, there is nothing more essential than the power of reason.

I recently found myself having to choose between a calm, reasonable response and an angry emotional response to my five-year-old James. I had just settled into my favorite reading chair after washing the dishes, wiping the table, and sweeping the floor after dinner. After about a page of reading, my daughter called me to come to the deck. I could tell by her voice something was wrong. James decided it would be a good idea, or at least fun, to spread ketchup around the deck and then jump in it. Just minutes after my cleaning-up, the deck, the chairs, the steps into the house, and James were splattered with ketchup. I was frustrated and angry. Instinctively, I wanted to yell at him and began to do so. But for some reason, on this occasion, unlike many other occasions, I caught myself, gained some composure, and tried to respond calmly. With a firm edge in my voice, I explained to James that spilling food is wasteful, makes the house a mess, and makes more work for everyone. To drive this point home, I insisted that he help me clean up the mess.

Most parents can probably identify with the feelings I had upon finding the place a mess. My frustration was due, in part, to having to clean up where I had just cleaned and being interrupted from the pleasure of reading a good book. My anger was the result, in part, of seeing James as careless or even inconsiderate. By interpreting the situation through these emotions I was well on the way to responding harshly.

When emotions are so strong that they overwhelm reason, they hold us in bondage and limit our options for responding. If I were completely overtaken by frustration and anger, I would have yelled at James and sent him to his room, as I sometimes do. In this case, however, reason was able to hold its ground in the initial moment of response. For reason to hold its ground it must be active rather than passive.

Most of us, most of the time, are passive with regard to our emotional lives. To be passive toward our emotions is to misunderstand what is causing them. It is to think that we are choosing and acting freely when our emotions and their causes are unwittingly driving our behavior. A passive reason responds to the world and makes decisions about the world with confused ideas. Spinoza saw this lack of understanding as the primary source of human suffering and bondage. In fact, in Spinoza's eyes the proper use of reason is the only way that human beings can alleviate suffering and experience freedom. Unlike so many of his philosophical counterparts, Spinoza does not see freedom as an inalienable birthright. For him, freedom is something we must earn. Rather than starting with freedom, we strive for freedom. The active and proper use of reason is what makes it possible for us to achieve freedom. Unfortunately, the task of achieving freedom is extremely difficult because the primary source of our bondage is the inadequate understanding of our emotions. In cultivating the power of reason, we can liberate ourselves from the power of the emotions, not by eliminating them, but by understanding them. Reason gives us the power to understand and understanding gives us power over our emotions or freedom.

As Spinoza presents it, the stakes are high. Either we cultivate the power of reason properly and liberate ourselves from the alienating power of unconscious emotions or we remain imprisoned by them. To be imprisoned by the emotions is to have little or no control over one's life. In fact, it is worse. Not only does one who does not understand his emotions lack control over his life, he is deceived into thinking that he has control. Spinoza (1982, Prop. 2, Part III) makes this point by way of comparison when he writes,

A baby thinks that it freely seeks milk, an angry child that it freely seeks revenge, and a timid man that he freely seeks flight. Again the drunken man believes that it is from the free decision of the mind that he says what he later, when sober, wishes he had not said. . . . So experience tells us no less clearly than reason that it is on this account only that men believe themselves to be free, that they are conscious of their actions and ignorant of the causes by which they are determined.

To be ignorant of those things that cause us to feel and act as we do is to be very vulnerable to poor decision making and great suffering. In the absence of a rational understanding of the causes of our behavior and of our appetites, we do things without knowing why we do them. Our emotions and appetites hold us in bondage. As I indicated above, the person who is prone to road rage every time a car changes lanes in front of him attributes the cause of his anger to the driver in front of him. This rage holds him in bondage and he drives recklessly to cut off the other driver or at least to get close enough for the driver to see which finger he raises in the other's direction. Similarly, the parent who too frequently responds to inconveniences in the house by yelling at his child attributes the cause of his anger to the child. But more careful reflection reveals that most often in these cases, as in many others, the immediate trigger that sparks the angry emotion is not the adequate or actual cause of that emotion. The immediate event, whether another driver or a child spilling ketchup around the porch, is often just a trigger to a deeper source of frustration or anger that resides in the person's emotional vault. The anger displayed in an act of road rage or by the parent that habitually yells at a child cannot be understood by observing the ostensible cause, the trigger. Such anger can only be understood adequately by tracing the causes back to other significant events and relationships that have built up a reservoir of emotion over time such that anger becomes one's dispositional response in familiar situations. To have such a reservoir of emotions without understanding, or trying to understand, how it came to be is to be in bondage to those emotions. Such misunderstanding, and the responses it generates, contributes to a life of suffering. In the case of the parent–child relationship, the suffering is not limited to the frustrated or angry parent; it is inflicted on the child.

As Miriam Greenspan (2003, pp. 2–3) points out in *Healing through the Dark Emotions*, this lack of emotional awareness and control, and the ignorance by which it is perpetuated, is a major source of human suffering. Suffering occurs when we move away from our realizing our potential, away from living in accordance with our own nature rather than moving toward full actualization. We achieve full actualization when we live in accordance with our own individual nature by intuitively understanding our place in the whole of reality, *God* or *Nature*. In failing to understand our emotions, we mistakenly think that we are in complete control of our lives, that our actions are the free choice of an independent ego. In this state of mind, we believe that our strength, our power for acting, originates entirely from ourselves. Spinoza, like Emerson, reminds us that we are a part of a larger whole. The better we understand our place in this whole, and allow the power of *God* or *Nature* to work through us, the more powerful we become. We move away from, or alienate this power, when we fail to understand the world and ourselves, in particular, our emotions, in a reasonable way. But to know ourselves in this way, to know what is causing us to feel so angry in particular situations, is to have the composure and control that is required to act as an adult rather than a child, the composure that children need their parents to have, we must develop reason by graduating from confused or inadequate ideas to clear and distinct ideas and finally to intuition.

My frustration upon being interrupted from reading could not be adequately understood by examining the particulars of the situation exclusively. I know this because there are many other times that my reading has been interrupted by my children without causing negative emotions. An adequate understanding of my frustration requires a deeper understanding of its causes. For instance, the fact that I was behind on my work with deadlines looming likely contributed to my feelings of frustration at having to take time to clean up again. Without considering causes of my emotions other than James, I could not adequately understand them. As long as I misunderstood them, I would focus on James as their sole cause. And as long as I saw James as their sole cause, James would be the sole target of the response they generate. A five-year-old child is defenseless against an adult who is acting on the basis of misunderstood emotions. This is why it is so critical for parents to rely on an active reason in response to emotional situations rather than letting the emotions dominate our responses to children.

The transition from the confused ideas of a passive mind to the clear and distinct ideas of an active reason is magical. Once reason becomes active and makes the initial step of trying to understand why one is feeling anger, instead of merely reacting with anger, one transforms his emotional landscape. The power of reason to achieve freedom from emotional bondage is felt *as soon as* one uses reason to better understand the causes of an emotion. That is, as soon as I step back to ask the question, "why is spilt ketchup making me so angry?" I have already begun to wrestle free from the power the emotion has over me. Just by asking the question, by making reason active, I transform my relationship to my emotion and to James. I give myself some psychological space, some freedom, in which I am not compelled to act on my anger. Once I initiate the process of trying to understand my emotions, I am no longer at the mercy of them and neither is my child. This process, if pursued with care and vigilance, is likely to lead to some difficult truths from the past, i.e., what actually led to the buildup of anger. But it also reveals that my child is not the adequate cause of my anger. As a result, I am able to redirect my anger away from James.

In this case, the displacement of James as the sole or central cause of my negative emotions made it possible to explain to him why it is not acceptable to deliberately spill the ketchup. An emotional response would have made him feel bad for doing it, but would not have explained to him why he was feeling bad. In some cases, this might be all we can hope to accomplish. For instance, if a child is too tired to listen to explanations or places himself in danger by not listening, it may be appropriate to send him to his room and explain later. Being reasonable means responding appropriately. It does not always mean compromising, capitulating, or even negotiating. A reasonable parent understands that he is responsible for making the rules and enforcing them, even if it makes children upset. But establishing and enforcing rules should be done rationally, not from within the clouded confines of powerful emotions.

Furthermore, if we are satisfied with emotional responses, we will never learn what is motivating and determining our own behavior. We will never be able to develop our own personalities beyond the habitual responses that have been formed over the course of a lifetime. We will be condemned to repeat the emotional patterns and responses that are already in place. In families, this means subjecting children to the misunderstood frustrations and scars of their parents. Hence, not only is the one who does not adequately understand the causes of his emotions in bondage, those in his care are subject to the negative effects of such a life.[1]

We understand when a parent responds from the throes of emotion, but the reasonable response is almost always more effective in teaching children and certainly more insightful for the adult who tries to understand his emotions. Such understanding not only makes it possible to teach children what they need to know, it makes it possible for parents to find the source of their own strength, to learn who they want and need to be.

How Reason Overcomes Emotion

To argue for the importance of reason in understanding and controlling the emotions is not to suggest that a person with a well-cultivated reason doesn't have emotions or ignores them. As we know from almost all schools of modern psychology, to ignore or deny emotions is likely to lead to poor emotional health. The real power of reason lies in its ability to overcome negative emotions by reassociating or reconnecting them within a deeper or larger context. Spinoza (1982, Prop. 2, Part V) describes this process as follows: "If we remove an agitation of the mind, or emotion, from the thought of an external cause and join it to other thoughts, then love or hatred towards the external cause, and also vacillations that arise from these emotions, will be destroyed." An emotion is an affect of the body accompanied by the idea of that affect as its cause. Reason has the ability to work with these ideas and influence or even control the way emotions affect us.

To help illustrate how this process can work, we might think of it by way of an analogy with the computerized maps we use to get directions or locate a site. These maps are easily brought into lesser or greater focus. We can zero in on a specific street address or we can look at the general map of a country. If one were to come upon a computerized map left on the screen by a previous user that was focused only on a street address, it would not have much significance for the viewer. It could be a street in almost any town, city, or country. This would be analogous to an emotion that was so narrowly understood that the person experiencing the emotion does not understand where it came from or what it might lead to. We can remove an agitation of the mind, however, by joining it to other thoughts. This is analogous to reducing the focus of the computerized map so that the specific street address originally shown is connected with other streets around it. By panning out to get a broader view of the map, we can see what town or city the street is in. Once we see the street in a larger context, it takes on greater meaning for us. Similarly, reason has the capacity to connect an agitation of the mind, an emotion, with other thoughts and experiences. In so doing, the intensity of the agitation is diminished as we come to understand it better in a deeper or broader context.

The capacity of reason to connect ideas and perceived causes of the emotions can be powerful. To test this ability of reason in relation to the emotions, consider the powerful emotion of hatred. Hatred can be understood as a painful feeling accompanied by the idea of the cause of that pain. A person who lost a loved one in the attacks of 9/11, for example, may feel intense anger or hatred toward Osama bin Laden. As long as one attributes the cause of his pain to bin Laden, he is likely to feel hatred toward him. Hatred is a negative emotion, however, and negative emotions move us toward a state of less perfection. That is, they diminish our power for acting. If he is unwilling or unable to get beyond identifying bin Laden as the sole cause of his pain, he is likely to be consumed by hatred. On the other hand, if he can use reason to make other associations, he can remove the agitation caused by his loss, even in the midst of sorrow and pain. For instance, instead of focusing on bin Laden, he may focus on why the loss is so painful and remember why the person was so important in his life. This may lead him to think about the positive qualities of the person who was killed. Or it may lead him to try to understand the deeper causes of terrorism. As one gains a more complex understanding of world history and politics, the intense focus on a single terrorist dissipates. The active use of reason in trying to understand an emotion and the situations that generate emotions help us to overcome the agitations emotions cause. This is the power reason has over the emotions. By actively removing or diminishing negative emotions, we increase and deepen the power of our *conatus*, our ability for self-realization in the reality of *God* or *Nature*.

We have seen that this power can be extremely useful for parents in the context of family life. If a parent became accustomed to using reason in this way to contextualize and better understand the actions and motivations of children as well as the agitations of his own emotional life, he could contribute to a positive family environment characterized by freedom and understanding rather than the frustration and suffering that coincide with emotional bondage. The agitations that go along with the mishaps and frustrations of interacting with children, who often respond to the world spontaneously without rational deliberation, become less contentious, less hostile if the parent can actively understand the causal history of the child's behavior. Or when appropriate, the parent can turn the power of active reason on himself to better understand his own emotional landscape thereby diminishing the negative agitations that are so familiar in family life. In this way, even in the tight confines of familial ties, we can begin to move toward an experience of freedom.

Such freedom and fulfillment will be fleeting, however, if reason doesn't remain active and continue to clarify the context of the lives of children and the causal history of our emotions. Achieving an adequate understanding of how our emotional lives have been formed and how they continue to affect our lives requires that we open some of our most personal and painful experiences to rational scrutiny. On the one hand, to study one's personal life can be far more painful than studying a highly rational and ordered discipline like mathematics. On the other hand, since we are a part of nature and subject to the same laws that govern all of reality, we can study the emotions in the same way that we would study physics or mathematics, with a cool, detached rationality. Studying mathematics and emotions is similar because both forms of inquiry use reason to understand causal connections and such understanding makes it possible to escape the bondage of emotional life and to realize the full power of one's own personality or *conatus*.

The Unspoken Faith of a Rationalist

The philosophical psychology that arises out of Spinoza's work is persuasive. Like my colleague, I can easily see how it works once one has made a commitment to finding a reasonable understanding of the causes of our emotions or a child's behavior. The question that arises with such work is what enables one to choose the path of reason. What will make a parent step back from the anger while it is happening? Reason can only work if one chooses to use it. My response to James spilling ketchup could easily have been dominated by anger in which case I would have explained nothing and sent him to his room. It often is. If I had a more developed understanding of my underlying emotional life, however, I would be less inclined to respond with negative emotions. And like so many parents, I often find my emotions getting the better of reason. The goal of philosophical faith and of faith in reason is to cultivate an understanding and a disposition that does not get overwhelmed by emotions. Such a disposition has the intuitive insight that is necessary to make wise decisions.

It is difficult to achieve such a disposition. As Spinoza (1982, Prop. 42, Part V) reminds us at the conclusion of *The Ethics*, "If the road I have pointed out as leading to this goal seems very difficult, yet it can be found. Indeed what is so rarely discovered is bound to be hard." It is so difficult in fact that theologians recognize it as God's work. From a religious point of view, we cannot save ourselves, only God can save us. Spinoza, in contrast, promises that one who has cultivated reason to the level of intuition will experience "blessedness," "glory," "salvation," "freedom," and an "intellectual love of God" (1982, Part V). These are the experiences the person of religious faith hopes for as the reward for a life well-lived in devotion to God. But he does not expect to achieve these experiences on his own. He prays for God to intervene and save him out of mercy and compassion. For Spinoza, individuals have the ability to experience the intensity of religious blessedness as the result of the proper cultivation of reason.

For the rationalist, these experiences occur because we have used reason to attune ourselves to *God* or *Nature* and in doing so, we realize our own true nature. We become aware of the divine presence in the world and of ourselves as a mode of that presence by understanding the particulars of the world, especially the particulars of our own lives such as our emotions. The better we understand the specifics, the better we understand God. This is intuition, the highest way of knowing. Intuitions give us an understanding of the whole by understanding parts in their proper context.

For parents, the mere possibility of achieving intuition can be powerful. When we are disposed to anger or frustration, we can remind ourselves that our misunderstood emotions are preventing us from seeing our children and ourselves in the context of *God* or *Nature*. This simple reminder is often enough to activate reason, to begin the search for a clearer understanding of the meaning in what is taking place. And once that search begins, the emotional landscape is altered with positive emotions replacing negative ones.

Spinoza's unspoken faith is a faith in reason. For him, salvation and blessedness are not the gifts of a merciful God to be dispensed to believers in the next life. They are at our disposal in this life if we make the effort to cultivate reason properly. The experience of blessedness and freedom is the result or the payoff of a life devoted to a rational understanding of the world and one's place in it. Whereas the primary responsibility of the religious person is faith and devotion to God, the responsibility of the rationalist is to develop and use reason well. As in religious life, however, a life devoted to reason requires faith because there are precious few examples of people who have successfully persisted in such a life. As a result, we do not know if devotion to a life of reason will achieve the benefits described by philosophers until we have tried it for ourselves.

Hence, faith in reason and religious faith both require the courage to take risks. Whereas religious faith is a risk to commit oneself to a belief in a mysterious, unseen, and unknown God, faith in reason requires a commitment to cultivating the capacity of reason which, in turn, requires that we sacrifice much of what is accepted in contemporary society. Before we can graduate to the level of intuition where we experience the payoff of blessedness and salvation, we must persist in forging out logical sequences to explain and understand the world. There is hard work to be done in resisting the spontaneous scream at a child when we are feeling stress from the demands of work. It is exhausting to demand and provide logical explanations in dialogue with those who are not committed to such clarity. In making the effort to realize reason's full capacity, however, we will find clues along the way to encourage the pursuit. For instance, the parent who tries to understand his emotions in a situation that he would ordinarily express anger will experience the pleasure of freedom that occurs whenever reason is active. This is the magical part of reason and the pursuit of understanding that is experienced along the way, before we achieve blessedness.

Faith is a prerequisite for acting rationally. We will make the effort to resist the spontaneous, emotional response only if we believe that a rational response will not only be more effective for the child and for the dynamics of the family, but also that it will be more satisfying for the parent, even in the short term. The frustration of not getting things done, or having to do them repeatedly because our children undo what we have done, or the frustration of being ignored by our children often makes us want to throw our hands up and scream. But when we find ourselves with rare moments of peace, if we reflect on what is most effective for everyone involved, we will begin to see the power and the benefits of reason as a means of responding to difficult and irrational situations. Over time, these insights will foster a disposition that is pervasive and persistent. With such a disposition, parents can understand the motivations of children as well as the emotions that drive us. This understanding and the disposition it supports empower us to direct our own lives instead of having them unconsciously directed by our emotions. For parents and for children, this power is the difference between a life that is, for the most part, peaceful and a life of contentiousness in the home.

Note

1. See *The Drama of the Gifted Child: The Search for the True Self* by Alice Miller for a detailed analysis of parents imposing their misunderstood emotions on their children in what she describes as "cycles of contempt."

CHAPTER FIVE

FAITH AND FREEDOM
OR FAITH IN FAITH

Without a clear sense of direction, values, and goals, it is easy to lose sight of what we are trying to accomplish as parents. It often feels as if we are running with our heads down, turning quickly to avoid obstacles, but failing to see the direction in which we are moving. As time passes, and it passes quickly, we look up to see that we have arrived far away from where we had expected to be. Along the way we don't recognize that we are moving off course because it seems as if we are freely directing our lives in response to the world. We engage in conversation with our peers and express our points of view, but we sometimes fail to recognize that the conversations in which we participate determine what we will talk about. They set the limits and provide a context for what can be meaningfully expressed. It is too late when we recognize that our participation in a particular conversation has led us to talk about things that pull us away from our values and goals. We tend to deceive ourselves into thinking that we are forging our own path by engaging in the give and take of each day when in reality we are progressing like two people sailing on a boat, too preoccupied with each other to look up, while the tide pulls as off course. If we do not reflect on our habits of thinking and acting and on our conversations, activities, and friends, we can be carried away from our true values and goals by the tide of social acceptance.

Being pulled off course is a very real danger for parents who are faced with so many pressures to move in different directions. Insofar as we succumb to these pressures, we diminish our ability to direct our lives and to adequately guide our children. Children are looking to us for direction, even if their incessant demands and tirades say otherwise. To provide that direction, we need to know where we want to lead them, what values we want them to live by, and which ideals we want them to aspire to. To do this, we need to *believe* in our values and goals; but we must also *believe* that it is *worthwhile* to resist the trends, expectations, and comforts that conflict with our goals and values. For instance, parents may know the value of cooking healthy food and sharing dinner as a family, but the pace of everyday life makes the convenience of take-out too alluring to resist. Instead of a time to share food and stories, dinnertime becomes an exercise in expediency and pulls us away from what we value.

Many parents find the patterns and habits of everyday life too strong to resist. Because these habits and patterns are so familiar, it is often easier to accept them as our fate, as our only possibility, than it is to change them. In fact, we often see better alternatives to the way we are raising our children, but as long as our *belief* in these alternatives lacks sufficient strength they will not become our reality. To adopt an alternative way of relating to the world and to others, in particular, our children, requires us to change deeply entrenched habits of thinking and acting. This kind of change requires sacrifice. Sacrifice involves hardship. And we will voluntarily endure hardship only if we *believe* the alternative we are pursuing is *worthwhile*. Without this belief, we will continue to gaze at the alternatives like a spectator who watches the game but never plays. For those with an inadequate belief in themselves and in the worthiness of change, alternative styles of parenting become something for others to pursue. Without the *belief* that alternatives are possible and worth pursuing, the other dimensions of philosophical faith are ineffective.

Each dimension of philosophical faith—faith in self, faith in the world, faith in the child, and faith in reason—presents an opportunity for development. But such development only occurs by overcoming substantial obstacles. Whether self-doubt, misunderstood emotions, or the pressure of social expectations, the antidote needed to resist these obstacles begins with the *belief* that there are alternatives to unsatisfactory, socially driven approaches to parenting and that we have the power to find or create these alternatives.

The final dimension of philosophical faith, then, is the primal underlying belief that the payoff for developing oneself, pursuing one's best ideas, cultivating reason, and believing in the latent capacities of developing children will lead to a better life, even if it is a more challenging and difficult life. The *belief that it is worthwhile* to live by values that go against the grain of social norms and expectations is the essential precursor to finding the autonomy and freedom parents need to authoritatively guide their children toward healthy adulthood. Without this preliminary dimension of faith, we are likely to feel stuck in our circumstances and patterns of living, unable to see the possibility of better alternatives. For those who are in such a position, and most parents are from time to time, an awareness that we are free to choose our own possibilities, an awareness that accompanies the underlying dimension of philosophical faith, needs to be recovered. While such a recovery does not provide a clear forecast of the outcomes that lie ahead, it does increase one's autonomy and freedom to direct her life and the lives of her children. The key to such a recovery is silence.

Silence

Having been raised in the Bronx and lived in New York for most of my life, autumn is as much about the Yankees heading for a playoff series as the changing colors of the leaves. On a recent Friday night, the Yankees were playing the Boston Red Sox in a game with playoff implications. I was delighted when my two daughters asked if they could watch the game with me. We were only one half inning into the game, however, when Anna, the younger of the two, decided it would be more fun to practice her piano than watch the game.

As an academic living in lower Westchester, the only affordable houses are ones in which rooms serve more than one purpose. The dining room used to be a bedroom in our house until we added bedrooms to the second level. The bedroom door still hangs at the entrance to the room, but ever since it has been used as a dining room, the door has never been closed. It also serves as the piano room.

Anna left the couch and walked deliberately into the dining room to sit at her piano. She played for about a half-hour repeating Yankee Doodle Dandy and a couple of other tunes several times. I listened intermittently, dividing my attention between the game and her tunes. By the end of her session, she played her simple tunes without a blemish—a significant, if minor achievement.

I found what she did after playing more significant. She closed the top of the piano, put her music books away, turned out the light, and closed the door. I took notice because it was the first time that door had been closed in more than a year. As I gazed at the door, I came to realize that Anna was creating a silent space. It seemed as though she wanted a room that was quiet so that the notes of her tunes might fade peacefully into the background from which they emerged. Intuitively, she wanted to keep the noise from the television away from the echoes of her music.

A few days later, minutes after lying down to sleep, the phone rang. My wife answered. The expression on her face turned to dismay as she repeated the message she had just heard, "She passed away." I sat up, knowing that it was her grandmother who passed away. On this particular day, my wife's mother was away from home and so we went to the grandmother's home. We stood by her bed as she lay still. We prayed and as I tried to offer support to my wife as she mourned her grandmother's passing, I noticed myself looking at the blankets that covered her. I was anticipating the gentle rise and fall that accompanies a breath, but the blankets were still. I gazed at her nose and mouth, which was still open. They were still. I listened for the faint sound of a breath—silence. All the simple things I anticipate in the presence of a person laying in bed were absent. There was only silence.

When I talk to parents they want to know *how* we can recover philosophical faith, how they can find the conviction that it is worthwhile to cultivate and pursue alternative styles of parenting in the face of overwhelming pressure to conform. The single most important step in such a recovery is silence. I share these two stories of silence because I often find it hard to be silent, to be still, to turn off the mind's chatter long enough for it to have an effect on me. I need tools or tricks that remind me to be silent and that show me how to be silent. To help myself I use images. For instance, I imagine the room that is full of silence when Anna finishes playing the piano and closes the door. The light is turned off and the dark takes over, the sound stops and it becomes quiet. Visualizing the contrast helps—light turning dark, sound turning silent. I then transfer the image of a silent room into the silence of my mind. I imagine my mind becoming as quiet as the room and it does.

Standing by a person who has passed away only minutes before is not a trick to silence the mind. It is a reminder. When the breathing stops, all of our possibilities end. Whatever course we have taken is decided. We can no longer look up from the floor of our boat to navigate a different course. There is no more navigating to be done. But while we are still breathing we can change course. Not only can we look up to see where we are heading, we can alter our course. We can step back from the conversation to hear what is being said, to hear the topics of conversations, and most importantly, to hear what we ourselves say. By stepping back, we gain a perspective that is not available while we are engaged in the conversation. In silence, we can decide if engaging in the give and take surrounding the prevailing topics of conversation will lead us in the direction we want to travel. Stepping back in silence frees us to choose our own possibilities instead of following possibilities that are determined unreflectively by conversations and events that precede our arrival. This is especially important for parents who are faced with the challenge of deciphering the moods and emotions that motivate the words and deeds of their children. As they move from one developmental stage to the next, their perception of parents changes without any warning to the parent. As their perceptions change, their feelings and attitudes change. If a parent does not cultivate a reflective and composed disposition, his responses are likely to fuel the unpredictable and often unpleasant emotional outbursts of children and adolescents. On the other hand, if a parent honors himself and his child with significant moments of silence, he will have a better chance of seeing the child's behavior as a developmental phase and not a personal attack. It is this kind of insight that enables us to have faith that, in spite of how children may behave toward their parents at different times during the developmental stages of childhood and adolescence, they will be mature, well adjusted, and happy adults.

The recovery of philosophical faith, then, begins by honoring the self with significant periods of silence from which we can see more clearly the direction in which we are traveling and leading our children. Many of us fail to honor ourselves with such silence because we are afraid of what silence might reveal to us about ourselves, about the choices we make, and our motivations for making them. We are afraid that the affirmations that we seek in order to sustain the ego will ring hollow. And we are worried that such hollowness will not support our existence.

These fears may be warranted. The ego may be looking for support and affirmation in the wrong places. But once we allow ourselves to grow quiet and face up to the misguided pursuits of the ego, we will find that life is not empty behind the hollowness of social affirmation. Silence is not without meaning. It is not an annihilation of the self. It is not empty. In fact, it is behind the chattering concerns of the ego that we find our truest selves, our most important developmental needs, and the resources to live an authentic life. We need to become silent and still to recover the meaning and resources that reside in the silent dimensions of the self. In this stillness we will discover a world full of possibilities and the autonomy to chart the course on which we are most true to ourselves and to our children. It is *in* the meaning of this silent world that we can have faith. And it is *out* of this silent world that we recover the autonomy and authenticity that is required to be an effective parent.

Silent Reversibility

In order to know what to expect from a retreat into stillness and silence, we can look back to when we were silent and to those parts of our lives that continue to function in silence. We all begin life silently in the womb. But this silence is full of activity. The activity of the silent dimension of the self is experienced as a reversibility of the flesh—the flesh of the mother and the fetus. The fetus develops out of its embryonic simplicity by sharing the mother's bloodstream. This intertwined relationship grows and deepens for nine months and undergoes a transformation at birth. After birth the child breathes with its own lungs and has its own cardiovascular pulse but continues to be fed by the mother and held in her arms rather than in her womb. The intertwining of mother and child develops and deepens emotionally and psychologically as they become more independent physically. The silence of the reciprocal relationship in the womb, where vast amounts of intergenerational information is transmitted in the form of DNA, evolves into the ever-deepening quiet complexity of psychological and emotional relations as they grow in the world.

Unlike the experience of the womb, however, in which the child relates exclusively with the mother, after birth our reversible relationships are expanded to include and depend on the world in which we live. The structure of the reversible relationship of fetus and mother in the womb is carried forth and unfolded throughout our lives in an expanded horizon of relationships that go beyond the primary caregivers. For instance, air enters the lungs and we reciprocate with carbon dioxide. Food is ingested and we process the nutrients it contains so that they will be dispersed throughout the body through the blood and used as energy. Like plants that turn to the sun, absorb water and nutrients from the soil, and prepare themselves for rest when in the twilight of the day, we depend on the intuitive intelligence of the body to interact with the world in order to sustain our existence. As children grow into adults and gain independence from their parents, they deepen their dependence on an expanded network of reciprocal relationships with the human and nonhuman world.

This evolution indicates that from the beginning and throughout our lives, human beings are made for relationships. And from the beginning, the silent relationships in which we exist provide us with the information and tools we need to flourish in the world. A recent report issued by the Institute for American Values and Dartmouth Medical School (see Commission on Children at Risk, 2003, p. 15) confirms the philosophical insight that at the core of human nature we are made for interpersonal relationships. The need for healthy interpersonal relationships is not just born out of social circumstances, this need is programmed into our genes. This is stated in the first two points of their ten-point summary when they write

1. The mechanisms by which we become and stay attached to others are biologically primed and increasingly discernible in the basic structure of the brain.
2. Nurturing environments, or lack of them, affect gene transcription and the development of brain circuitry.

Just as a fetus' healthy development depends on a healthy environment in the womb, the healthy development of children requires healthy reciprocal relationships in the world. Without nurturing relationships, the unfolding of their genetic and cultural inheritance in the world will be abbreviated, feeble, grasping, confused, and chaotic. Genes are not permanently fixed, completely determined parts of a machine. As they unfold in the world, they adjust to their environment. If they unfold in a nonnurturing, hostile environment their potential for flourishing is curtailed. Like a plant that is deprived of healthy soil, they will grow unhealthy and wither.

The report also shows that, for a growing number of children, there is a significant deterioration of the nurturing relationships required for their healthy development. Despite dramatically improved material conditions over the past two decades, the authors write that "U.S. young people not only appear to be experiencing sharp increases in mental illness and stress and emotional problems, but also continue to suffer from high rates of related behavioral problems such as substance abuse, school dropout, interpersonal violence, premature sexual intercourse, and teenage pregnancy" (p. 9).

These are the behavioral trends of alienated youth who are searching for meaning and value in their lives, but searching in the wrong places. There are many factors contributing to these trends such as unstable home environments, the economic demand for two-income homes, the overstimulation of electronic media, and a tacit acceptance of violence and aggression in all sectors of society. These are significant obstacles to overcome if parents are to guide their children toward healthy adult life. But there will always be unhealthy social and cultural trends that children and their parents must resist. A parent's strength to resist these trends is born out of a faith that such resistance is possible and worthwhile. In order to recover this faith, or find it for the first time, it is helpful to understand the dynamic that is unfolding in the silent depths of our personalities and the personalities of our children.

I recently came across a photograph of a father lying on his stomach, supporting his upper body on his elbows with his infant son between them. The father is looking directly into his son's eyes from inches away. His son is reciprocating the gaze, while trying to push the rounded back of his partially closed miniature fist into his mouth, his legs curled up under his father's chest. Both are smiling, though each smile seems to convey something different. The father's smile is happy, serene, and appreciative. It reveals emerging wrinkles at the corner of his eyes, which contribute something extra to the smile. The child's smile is happy without restraint. It is a smile of tickled anticipation as if he is about to laugh. He is having fun looking at his father while lying between his large, coddling, and secure forearms.

The infant, whose joyful smile is reciprocated in the gaze of his father, is learning that his world is a welcoming, secure, and happy place. In this case, the reciprocity that is experienced in the womb at the beginning of life is being carried forth into the world in a positive way between father and son. As our interpersonal and reversible relationships grow more complex, our dependence shifts from an exclusively physical one to emotional, psychological, social interdependence. If these relationships are healthy, that is, if parents provide a safe, nurturing loving environment, the child learns to trust the world. Armed with a primal sense of trust, the child's initial response to others is not one of fear but of openness, curiosity, and welcoming. Openness and welcoming become the basis of a healthy personality because these qualities make it possible and likely that the child will feel safe in the world. If a child feels safe she will be more inclined to explore and take initiative than a child who is fearful (see Erikson, 1980). An infant that is not loved, not welcomed, coddled, and smiled at will learn that the world is not such a safe place and the building blocks of his personality will lack the essential quality of trust.

Without a basic sense of trust, it is difficult for the child to develop the higher stages of a healthy personality such as autonomy and initiative.

In order to avoid conveying destructive messages to children, especially in early childhood, it is helpful to remember that parents and children are looking at different worlds. The experience of early childhood is often seen as a period of enchantment. Unlike the world of adults who can use reason and thought to separate themselves from the world, the child's world is seen and experienced without the preconceptions of a rational mind. They don't anticipate, judge, and categorize; they observe and explore. Children participate in the reversibility of mirroring relationships with extreme openness and malleability. If the mirroring process is to serve as the basis of a healthy personality, parents need to honor the enchantment of the early stages of a child's life and have faith in the developmental capacities of the child. To find the peace of mind that is required in order to honor the wonder of early childhood and to have faith in the developmental processes of children, we need to honor ourselves with periods of silence.

Silence enables us to hear the developmental needs of children. Parents of older children know that the uncontained joy in the smile of an infant is easily transformed into the unrestrained scream of "I hate you" or "you're stupid" in the toddler. A parent's still and silent composure allows us to hear the messages that are conveyed behind these piercing words and hysterical screams. If we do not cultivate the composure that comes from significant periods of stillness and silence, we are likely to get caught in knee-jerk responses to such pronouncements. Lacking attunement to the silent dynamics of the developmental process in the child, and their childhood interpretation of our role as parents, the insecurities of the ego make us vulnerable to the hurt that can accompany the harsh words of a child. But if we have faith in ourselves and in the resilience of the silent dimensions of the personality—the child's and our own—we know that there is always more being said than the specific words convey. If we listen carefully, we can hear those messages. In fact, if we listen long and closely enough, our children sometimes reveal them to us.

My son recently made a couple of unwelcome pronouncements that needed to be interpreted for a meaning other than the words that were actually conveyed. The first, less threatening complaint made in anger toward me was that I "canceled summer" and as a result, he wasn't able "to go to the pool to swim anymore." While the thought of having such power is alluring, I couldn't hold on to it for long because I had to figure out how to get a five-year-old to stop crying because he believed it was true. The more troublesome declaration came during the pre-bedtime ritual. I interrupted his play in order to get him ready for bed. This upset him and he yelled that he hated me. While I was helping him to get into his pajamas, I told him why he shouldn't use the "hate" word. He then went on to explain that he said it because he wanted to keep playing and I am the one who always makes him stop when it is time for bed. I don't always get those follow-up explanations because I don't always react so calmly and, even when I do, he doesn't always offer them.

After countless interactions like these, I've come to realize that the outcome is always better when I maintain my composure. If I respond with a calm explanation of why it is important to get sleep and why it is not acceptable to use bad words or even if I do not respond but stay silent, James inevitably becomes calm and gets to sleep much faster. If I lose my composure and yell, he cries and it prolongs the process. More importantly, James's responses mirror my responses, and over time, he will internalize my ways of speaking and responding to situations. As a parent, I need to remind myself that each interaction is also a lesson that is transmitted in conjunction with my words in silent gestures and in the temperament of tone and style.

And even if James does hate me for the moment, my responsibility as a parent does not change. I must still uphold the rules and set limits. In meeting my responsibility, I draw upon my faith in the resilience of his personality. While it is unpleasant to watch my son being upset, it is critical that what is unpleasant does not dictate procedures. Over time, he will recognize that brushing his teeth and getting to bed on time are important. He will want to do these things for himself. But he will only learn these things if we are consistent in enforcing rules. To maintain this consistency, we must also have faith in our rules and ourselves. We must trust that what we demand of him is good for him. But to have faith in ourselves and in our children, we must first believe that it is worthwhile to identify a set of values and beliefs and that it is worthwhile to adhere to them, even when it is difficult to do so. Without the belief in the *worthiness of our beliefs*, we are sure to have them over-run by the tirades of our children or the trends of our friends.

So philosophical faith begins with the belief that alternatives are possible and worthwhile. In order to find and develop this faith, we need to honor the self with significant periods of silence and stillness. This silence includes silencing the internal voice of the ego, which clings to noise and information out of fear of losing its identity or its worth. We have seen, however, that such silence does not render us empty. At the core of the personality, from the beginning of life in the womb and continuing throughout our lives is a silent, interpersonal, reversibility. It is in this reversibility that the resources for a grounded, authentic, and purposeful personality reside. Unfortunately, our society tends to place excessive importance on the individual. As a result, the ego's desire for acceptance often leads us to forget and neglect the reversible, interpersonal underpinnings of the self. When this forgetfulness takes root, parents lose faith in themselves and lose touch with the resources in the silent dimensions of the self that make it possible to find and create alternative approaches to parenting. To resist this forgetfulness, it is helpful to be aware of how its symptoms are manifest.

Hyperindividualism

While individuation is an essential part of the maturation process, our society tends to overemphasize its importance. As the child begins to think for himself and separate from his parents, he often resists or rejects the values and constraints of his parents. He longs for the independence to make his own decisions and views this freedom as a rite of passage into adulthood. In the transition from adolescent to young adult, there are difficult times because the child is trying to outgrow a lifetime of dependence on his parents. He tends to see his parents as restrictive and out of touch with the world in which he is independent. Hence the child can give significant periods of resentment toward the parent.

The desire for independence and the willingness to fend for oneself is an essential part of healthy socialization. During the transition toward independence, the child will often use social conventions to distinguish himself from his parents' ways of being. Unfortunately, so much of social convention today overemphasizes the prizes of individuality, making it the highest goal of socialization. But this is in conflict with the underlying structure of human nature. The tendency to forget the interpersonal reversibility at the basis of our personalities often results in hyperindividualism, which is characterized by selfishness, a lack of healthy concern for others, and for society as a whole. Feeling separated from others and from the deeper resources of the self and having relied on the perceptions and messages of others for its identity, the ego-self can feel vulnerable and unsure of itself, insecure in who it is and what it should be. This vulnerability can cause it to feel defensive, especially when its ideas or points of view are challenged or threatened. In trying to protect and preserve itself, the ego often sets itself up as an antagonist toward others. It tends to see itself in conflict with the world in its individuation.

For many the experience of alienation and the defensiveness it generates leads to an overly egoistic personality. Having internalized the thoughts, attitudes, and feelings of others toward me while the interpersonal underpinnings of the personality are wounded or forgotten, the egoist sees the purpose of others to be the mere fortification of his ego. In seeing the self in the other, the egoist reduces the other to the needs or ideas of his own world. He does not look at the other as a free and independent person with her own rights and dignity; he sees the other as a sounding board, a mirror whose purpose is to reflect, not to be seen. The narcissist looks at the other only to see himself. He becomes incapable of authentic and healthy interpersonal relationships because for the narcissist all others are seen as an opportunity, a way of advancing the interests of the ego-self. If the narcissist does not see any possibility for fortifying his ego in another, he does his best to avoid or minimize exposure to him.

This personality type does not make for good parenting for a number of important reasons. First, parents have a responsibility to purposively direct their lives and the lives of their children in accordance with ideals and values that are chosen by parents out of serious reflection. This entails a high level of self-awareness to know when we are being led by the values of others instead of our own values. Second, in order to adequately guide children, parents need to be able to hear the messages that are conveyed in the words and gestures of children. In order to hear these messages, we must be highly attuned to their lives and to the interpersonal structure at the core of our own lives. This attunement requires that we listen to them and to ourselves in silence and stillness. It requires that we put the ego and its desires in the context of the whole personality. With such attunement, we can better know the deepest concerns and motivations of our children and ourselves.

The egoist cannot be silent and still enough to hear. He cannot guide children in accordance with values of self-awareness because he deceives himself into thinking he acts freely when his actual reasons for acting are the ego's desire to fit into social trends and expectations. In reality, he loses his autonomy and his authenticity because his self-enclosed world does not allow for personal growth, discovery, or spontaneity. His lack of understanding and forgetfulness of the deeper structures of his personality render him passive and confined to a life determined by the winds of chance. In losing touch with the deeper resources of the personality, he loses the opportunity to direct his life and the lives of his children in accordance with the needs and desires of his deeper nature.

The negative consequences of the socialization process result in the isolation and loneliness of individuals, and by extension they are felt across society in the breakdown of civic responsibilities, communities, and simple neighborly courtesy and concern (Putnam, 2000; Bellah et al., 1985; Committee on Children at Risk, 2003). The distortion and alienation that one feels as a maladjusted ego-self not only closes him off from healthy interpersonal relationships with others, it also separates him from sources of meaning that lie beneath the socially derived concerns of the ego-self. Only by tapping into the silent source of meaning at the base of our personalities can one identify and grow in accordance with values and ideals that are in tune with our deepest and highest self. Healthy interpersonal relationships and the pursuit of substantive meaning beyond the concerns of the ego, both of which are hard-wired into our genes, are not possible without the autonomy that comes from a healthy sense of philosophical faith at the base of the personality. In devoting energy to protect and preserve the ego, we lose sight of our best possibilities; the possibilities that allow us to work toward becoming our truest and most fulfilled self. And it is the perils of the socialization process that cause us to lose touch with the quiet force and the autonomy of our philosophical faith.

So it is the silent reversibility of our relationships that provides the foundations of our personalities and the potential for who we can become. The messages that we convey to our children in these reversible relationships has the danger of going astray, but if we proceed with caution, they will be the basis of a child's healthy personal development. The autonomy we want for our children needs to include the development of meaningful interpersonal relationships. In fact, it depends on it. Autonomy is not found in isolation. We are always affected and shaped by others. The healthy adult recognizes that his autonomy is strengthened by his ability to live in accordance with the deepest structures of his personality, which are interpersonal to the core. To carry this nature forward into the world is to carry forth the values of empathy and understanding, concern for others, because we recognize that who we are is shaped by how we relate with others. To be human is to exist outside of ourselves by caring for others and by caring for ourselves.

The Autonomy of Faith

The primary goal of nurturing philosophical faith is to increase one's autonomy as a parent. Fortunately, we already have a trace of the faith we need, even if it is taken for granted, unrecognized, unfelt, and underutilized. To rediscover and nurture it, we need to listen attentively for its quiet force; otherwise the noise of life will drown it out. By carefully listening for what is at work and what is being neglected beneath the surface of our everyday lives, we can recover the strength and freedom of a healthy philosophical faith. By raising our awareness of this faith that we rely on all the time, but rarely pay attention to, we will increase the autonomy we need in order to enact alternatives to the obstacles that so often prevent us from raising healthy children.

In *The Dynamics of Faith*, Paul Tillich (1957) writes: "Faith is a matter of freedom. Freedom is nothing more than the possibility of centered personal acts" (p. 5). The free individual is one who plays an active role in directing his life. The obstacles to choosing what he wants to do with his life, whether those obstacles are self-doubt, incomplete understanding, or emotional turmoil do not overwhelm one who executes "centered personal acts." A person who is centered knows what he wants to do and why he wants to do it. He remains focused on his goal, even if he does not fully understand what it takes to achieve it or what its consequences will be. Life does not direct him; he directs his life.

Another way of looking at freedom, however, is to see it as the result, the payoff, of one who has gone through the difficult process of refining reason and liberating himself from misunderstood emotions. We all begin with confused ideas about the world and our place in it. With confused ideas, we are not in a position to live in accordance with our own truest nature. That is, with confused ideas, we tend to make mistakes. With a clear and rational understanding of self and the world, however, one is in a position to see how the world works and how we fit into that world. Over time, if we deepen our sense of place in the world, we begin to see things intuitively; that is, we come to see the meaning of the whole by way of the part. Intuition and freedom go hand in hand because the intuitive person can see his place in the whole and as a result he does not try to be something he is not. He does not resist what cannot be changed, but lives in accordance with his nature or the world in general. We have seen that for Spinoza, this is the highest perfection, the most complete experience of freedom we can have. At this level of understanding, one has liberated himself *from* the bondage of emotions. For one who has achieved this liberation life is blessed and the need for faith is minimal.

But for Tillich freedom is there at the start. It is the freedom *to* choose and act, not the outcome of a long and arduous process of intellectual refinement or the result of escaping *from* emotions. And yet even for Tillich, freedom is not something automatic, universally endowed to all human beings at all times. The freedom to choose one's possibilities is a centered act, which means it must be directed by an active self and not determined and driven by influences on a passive self. Only as the centered act of an active and autonomous individual "freedom and faith are identical" (Tillich, 1957, p. 5). They are identical because to be free is to *believe* that one has possibilities that have yet to be realized. With this belief, one can search for possibilities that have yet to be pursued or realized. Only with an awareness of what is possible will we be able to choose the direction of our lives, choose which possibilities we want to pursue and which we want to leave behind. If we do not *believe* we have any choices, any possibilities other than what fate has already thrown at us, then we are in fact not free. In the absence of belief there is an absence of possibility and a lack of freedom to choose.

So both faith and freedom are present at the beginning of a self-directed life and both can be cultivated and strengthened to contribute to an autonomous and fulfilled life. Even the person who feels stuck, as if fate has determined her life, relies on at least a trace of faith when she engages in the menial tasks of daily life. For instance, on some level, as with all living organisms, there is a will to live. This will to live is bound up with an underlying *belief* that life is worthwhile and that the future is worth hanging around for, even if the conscious mind does nothing but complain. In fact, we rely on some small level of faith in almost everything we do, from cooking breakfast to writing a book. In all of our endeavors, however mundane, we are buoyed by a primal belief that we can accomplish the task at hand and that it is worthwhile to do so. Unfortunately, for many, this faith has not been nurtured and cultivated. In some instances it has been damaged and its pulse has grown faint. Yet it is there. For these people, autonomy and freedom are minimal and they often feel stuck. Their underdeveloped faith does not have the strength or stamina to support the pursuit of higher endeavors and ideals. Their weakened faith limits them to taking on the menial tasks that life throws at them.

Feeling stuck is familiar to most parents. We often feel as if accomplishing daily chores such as feeding our children, helping them with their homework, and persuading them to get to sleep is the extent of our possibilities. In the midst of the seemingly endless cycle of tasks, it seems as if there is no time to direct life the way we would like. In meeting the demands of our children, we tend to loose sight of our own needs and ideals. In looking out for others we often lose touch with ourselves. We become the support staff of our children's emotional and social lives responding to their needs and to the demands of social expectations. In nurturing a healthy philosophical faith, we can effectively accomplish the tasks of parenting while also retaining a sense of autonomy and purpose in our lives.

SIMPLE STEPS TO PHILOSOPHICAL FAITH

As early as I can remember I helped my father with work around the house. In the beginning I was cleaning up pieces of wood and sheetrock, retrieving tools, or holding one end of a chalk line while he snapped it. He didn't like to work where there was dirt. So several times during a workday I was told to sweep the floor. His tools were put away in very precise order in his tool cabinet. Measurements had to be exact. As I got older, the responsibilities grew. I was barely a teenager when I was helping him lay out floor plans, frame out walls, and sheetrock them. In his spare time, he built houses. We did all of the work, from the footings to the finished trim.

I can hardly remember a time when my father stopped to show me how to do things. He expected me to know somehow. This made for many anxious moments while I thought through things in my head, often making believe I knew what I was doing while I was figuring it out. Not wanting him to know I didn't know how to do something, I was forced to learn quickly. I watched and listened, especially when he talked to his peers about how to organize and execute a job. For all of these jobs, his expectations were high. In working to meet those expectations, I gained a wealth of knowledge.

In the process of learning how to build and fix and plan, I acquired something much deeper and more formative from my parents. I learned or, more accurately, acquired a rhythm to my days. This rhythm is like an inner clock that tells me when it is time to work, when it is time for rest, and when it is time for a cup of tea. Like the equilibrium of health that our bodies seek in the process of healing from an illness or an injury, I am guided by a rhythmic ebb and flow around which I organize the activities each day. These rhythms began to develop in me as a child when I would watch my father leave the house each morning at about 6:30 and return home at 4:00. My mother would have dinner ready when he got home and we would eat by 4:30. On Saturdays we were always awake early, and if we did not have basketball practice or a game, we had jobs to do around the house. Sunday morning we went to Mass and then to Gaelic Park where we either played or watched Irish football and hurling games.

The patterns of our days and weeks were very consistent. In large part, this consistency was the result of my parents' faith in themselves and in their own interests. As Irish immigrants, they retained and cultivated a deep interest in Irish music and sports. We spent our childhood summers in Ireland, mainly because they wanted to go home. On Friday and Saturday nights we listened to Irish men and women tell stories in Irish and English and play music on fiddles and flutes in our living room. We were not asked to participate in these conversations. We listened and observed from the periphery. We were witness to adults pursuing and discussing their interests. We watched them interact in conversation, story, and music. We listened to unique interpretations of the events of the day from what was happening in the neighborhood to labor issues, religion, and politics. While we understood that we were the focus of our parents' intense devotion, we also knew that we were not the center of attention in these settings. Their faith in their own interests served as the basis of life lessons for us, their children. These lessons were absorbed as a means of social awareness and respect for others as well as a sense of belonging, not only to a family, but to a community and an ancient heritage. Confirming Aristotle's insight that we develop habits for living early in life, the ways of my parents provided me with an attraction for a style and rhythm to life that is not easily learned elsewhere. Without thinking about it, in pursuing their own interests, they transmitted a generational gift to their children that cannot be found in any store or on any website.

In remembering events from my childhood, I am not advocating a return to patriarchal dominance as an ideal family structure. I am, however, pointing to the importance of parents pursuing their own healthy interests in balance with providing opportunities for children to pursue theirs. A parent's lack of faith in him or herself can easily result in a conflation of child and adult interests. Such a conflation can be both confusing and overbearing for children and, ultimately, unfulfilling for parents. This conflation also can lead to a lack of identity and direction from within the home. When a child's activities are the sole interest of the family, it is the interests and activities of the community, i.e., someone else that directs family life and not the ideas and principles of the parents. In such a situation, the inner life and structure of the home is threatened.

As I reflect on the moods and energy of my days as an adult, I find that they closely mirror the patterns of my childhood. I am aware of a strong pull to waking at 6:30 and winding down my workday around 4:00. Dinner is usually later than 4:00 in our house, but I begin to think about finishing what I am working on at that time, even if I am required to work later. These unconscious rhythms are very powerful for me and I suspect they are for most of us. We absorb these patterns from the earliest days of our lives when we are most impressionable. These rhythms are not lessons communicated in words, we absorb them as naturally as the air we breathe and the foods we eat. While these rhythms are not fixed in stone and can be altered by consistently following alternative schedules, they are strong and slow to change. For me, they serve as a reference point for organizing my day.

I feel fortunate to have absorbed such a distinct daily rhythm. I find this inner reference point to be a central component of what it means for me to live well. If I ignore this inner rhythm too often, I feel out of sorts with myself and I work at trying to regain it. In today's working climate, a day that begins at 6:30 and winds down at 4:00 may seem like an unrealistic, romantic wish from the past. I am not suggesting that such a time frame is the only or even the optimal time frame for daily living. I must often work well beyond these hours. I am suggesting, however, that consistency in the daily lives of a family and children is important.

I often see the effects on people who were never exposed to consistent patterns of living. These effects often reveal themselves most powerfully in college students who are required to make and keep their own schedules for the first time. There are many influences that push college age students to keep unconventional hours. But students who have absorbed healthy or consistent patterns of living from home are best able to resist the pull to keep unconventional hours and when they do succumb to these pressures, they are better able to regain healthy patterns. These patterns give them a reference point against which they can measure their schedules. They know when and why they are run down and out of synch with their habits for sleeping, eating, and studying because they have something to be in synch with and they know how it feels to be in tune with their inner rhythm. For those students who come from homes in which there is little or no structure, it is much more difficult to find a healthy equilibrium because they have no internal rhythm to serve as a reference point. They are drifting from day to day and night to night without having cultivated a style or pattern to their day.

I introduce the notion of a daily rhythm in response to a very simple and direct question from my neighbor who generously took the time to read an early draft of this manuscript. She said that she understood and agreed with what the text was arguing, but she wanted to know what a parent was supposed to do about it. How do we put these ideas into practice? This is a familiar challenge that arises in response to philosophical thought, and I believe that philosophers do not spend enough time thinking about answers to this question. A typical philosophical response to such a question is that there is no one answer and each individual must find it for him or herself. There is truth in such a response. Nobody can say how a parent's philosophical faith should be manifest in the context of family life. One of the major points of being a faithful parent is that our decisions and actions must come from our deepest and highest selves and not follow the prescribed answers of others.

Nonetheless, it would not be irresponsible for a philosopher to go further and make some suggestions about practices that might be in line with a healthy sense of philosophical faith.

Are there things we can do in our homes, with our children, and with each other that naturally elicit and strengthen this faith? Establishing consistent rhythms of the day is one place to start. Children will absorb these rhythms and consciously or unconsciously refer to them throughout their lives as they negotiate the most effective way to live. More specifically, there are activities around which the rhythms of the day are formed that demonstrate and strengthen philosophical faith. As Miriam Weinstein (2005) brilliantly argues in *The Surprising Power of Family Meals*, cooking and eating meals together is one of them. So even if we are not rooted in a cultural tradition or lack a passionate interest to pursue from which our children can witness and learn a style of living, we need to eat. And how we go about this basic human need can become an oasis of common family interest and pleasure.

Among the many highlights of Weinstein's work is her insight into the dynamic effect of conversation among family members and the importance of children participating in the preparation of family meals. From simply being exposed to the vocabulary of adults to learning how to follow conversations as they jump from topic to topic, children who regularly eat meals with their family gain tangible and intangible advantages over those who do not. For instance, when children hear words at the dinner table that they later come across in a book for the first time, it is much easier for them to figure out its meaning than if they had never heard it before. Moreover, children who are accustomed to following adult conversations have an easier time adjusting to unfamiliar social situations. But beyond these tangible advantages of conversing with adults at mealtime are the comfort, security, and intimacy that come from a predictable mealtime.

One of the challenges parents and children face today is the frenetic pace of life that is fueled by the vast amount of activities available to children and families. These activities are often scheduled during evening mealtime. Families are rushing from soccer to theater to music lessons. In themselves, these are good activities. And yet, they can become destructive when they overwhelm family life and eliminate the interactions that occur at mealtime. Parents must weigh the overall benefit to the child when their days do not include quiet time and a healthy meal where family members communicate and discover what each is thinking about and feeling. Weinstein points out that even the teenager who wears the look of disdain, as if sitting at dinner is screwing up her evening, really wants to be there. She wants to know that when she needs support or advice or admonishment, her mother or father or both will be there to give it to her. Young children need to learn the social mores of community which includes listening as well as talking and cleaning up after oneself. To participate in the mechanics of preparing and cleaning up after a meal are not hardships for children, despite what they may say from time to time. In fact, as Weinstein points out, the more responsibility we give them in these situations the more they like it.

Okay, I too was suspicious when I read this. So I decided to test it out. First of all I wanted to see if it was possible to get my children interested in preparing a dinner and then, if it was, would it have a positive effect on mealtime. My son James is a finicky eater. I wondered if having him participate in the meal would change his attitude toward the food. I went to Randazzo's fish market on Arthur Ave. in the Bronx to buy some fresh fish. When I got home, I asked my children if they wanted to help prepare dinner. They all did and, to my surprise, James was the most enthusiastic. The duties that can be assigned to a five-year-old are limited, but since the girls did not want to handle the fish, he decided it would be brave of him to do so. When I asked if he would help me prepare the fish, he (literally) jumped at the chance. I helped him place the filets on the baking pan and then put the pan into the oven. He loved the slimy feel of each fish as he moved them from the dish on the counter to the baking pan. All three helped to set the table and the dinner was ready a short time later. If I was not there, I would have had a hard time believing the response at the dinner table. James was as enthusiastic to eat his fish as he is at birthday parties when the cake arrives. He ate two servings of sole, something he would usually cry about without ever tasting it. There really is a surprising power to family meals.

Weinstein confirms, unfortunately, the sociological data showing that family mealtime is under siege in middle-class America. As parents push their children to fill their resumes with soccer, dance, and service at soup kitchens while taking college exam preparation courses, there is little time left for family dinners. Fast food is gobbled down in the car en route from one activity to another. In fact, Weinstein discovered in her travels around the country that it is not uncommon to find homes in which there is no dining table. The physical effects of poor eating habits are being registered across the country with significant increases in obesity and related disease such as diabetes. But there are other effects as well. One of these is the quiet but dependable rhythm we come to rely on in organizing our days that is lost on children when parents do not have a rhythm of their own. In looking for a way to cultivate and exercise the power of philosophical faith, making dinnertime a family affair might be a place to start.

But the family meal is just one example of how parents can begin to recover the faith they need to provide the example and leadership their children need. While social pressures tell us and our children that we should sign up for another clinic, or workshop, or tryout, or practice, we need to *believe* in the simple power of being together as a family on a regular basis. We need to trust in ourselves, in the structure of family life, and in the underlying ability of children to find pleasure in the close, quiet activities of the home. We need to have faith that the dynamics of these times together will have lasting benefits on the character of our children throughout their lives. It always helps, of course, if there is pleasure associated with a regular meeting and food can certainly be such a pleasure. But there are plenty of other pleasures that can emerge if we give ourselves a chance. In order to reclaim family time and the benefits associated with it, parents need to believe in themselves and their children. In the face of their children's resistance and disdain even, they need to trust that the simple, quiet activity of sharing a meal or a story is pleasant, healthy, and sometimes more important than being involved in yet another activity outside the home. They must also trust that their children will come to realize the importance of such activities at some point in their lives, even if they cannot see it or understand it now.

Underlying Challenges to Parenting

Against the backdrop of what concerns a lot of parents, emphasizing consistent family meals might seem simplistic, if not naïve. Parenting is difficult today and much of what makes it difficult seems to be beyond our control. For starters, we must compete with the media—the modern-day storytellers—and the messages they convey about what is important and how to live. From the beginning, philosophers understood the importance of the stories told to children. Plato and Aristotle both recognized that the character of children is formed before they can think for themselves as they identify with the characters and plots of the stories they see and hear. This is where they develop the notions of good and bad and the attractions and interests they will pursue throughout their lives. When we step back to see and hear the stories that form the backdrop of the world in which we are raising our children, we realize that our challenges are great.

For instance, a pervasive theme in American media is violence. It is in the animated shows that children watch, it is in their video games, and it dominates newscasts. We regularly hear about murder and threats to our security while the United States is engaged in wars with no end in sight. Our leaders try to minimize the horrors of war, and parents struggle to shield our children from them.

In addition to the insecurity and doubt of living with violence and war in the background of our days, we are faced with the burden of a political culture in which dishonesty, corruption, and scandal have become acceptable. These developments breed a lack of trust in our leaders at a time when strong, principled leadership is required. If we are going to effectively address the major issues of our time, issues that will have decisive impact on the lives of our children and grandchildren, we need leaders that can look beyond the next election cycle. In the meantime, public policy continues to chip away at the needs of parents and families. Wages and pensions are deteriorating along with the environment and the air we breathe. Funding for education is being cut while pork spending is stuffed into bills hidden behind the façade of national security. Communities on which parents could depend in the past to assist in the process of raising children are deteriorating and are replaced with increasing isolation. These are serious problems that seem beyond the power of individual parents to address.

And here I am talking about having dinner together. But before laughing off such a simple suggestion, we might do well to remind ourselves that few of us have the power to affect the world, or even small aspects of it, on a major scale. As a group, parents have the best opportunity to affect change on a small, incremental basis. In order to affect positive change, however, parents cannot continue to be mesmerized by the media in the form of advertisers, insincere politicians, or an overbooked activities schedule. In order to resist these powerful messages and temptations, parents need to have philosophical faith. They must believe in themselves so that they can, first, discover their own principles for living and then act on those principles. They must also believe in their children, trusting that they have the mettle to find meaning and purpose in higher callings; that they can, in fact, defer gratification for a higher reward in the future; that they can find the pleasure and enjoyment of sticking with a project or an activity over time, even if it is boring or hard at times. Parents need to remind themselves of the resilience of children and direct that resilience to take on their higher challenges. Parents also need to trust in the hidden meanings and coherence of the world itself. While we are inundated with disappointing, sometimes tragic news on a regular basis, we are also in the presence of order, meaning, and beauty on a regular basis. If we believe in the order, meaning, and beauty of the world, even when we don't see it so clearly, we can seek it out, find it, and live with it. In doing so, we need to trust in and cultivate the powers of reason. Reasonable thinking is a unique gift of the human species. It can be used for good or bad. But in the context of family life, where so much is communicated in the prerational domain, parents can benefit themselves and their children by relying on sound reason as often as possible. Faith in oneself, the world, children, and reason are the critical dimensions of philosophical faith that can help initiate a healthy path for our children and our families. And to get started, we need the faith that it is worthwhile to pursue these different dimensions of faith.

Philosophical faith is humble. It recognizes that we have the ability to change only small things. It doesn't promise the hope of salvation, just the hope of being able to do things differently. There is strength in this little bit of hope, in the belief that it is worthwhile to look beneath the surface of the world and oneself to explore our options. Faith in the worthiness of small changes is supported by the knowledge that small changes are the easiest to sustain and changes that are sustained become a way of life. For parents, these changes can begin in their homes, with those they are closest to, and for whom they are responsible.

In thinking about change, it is helpful to remind ourselves that it is often ineffective to just say no to things we want to change. Change is more effective and sustainable when we replace an undesirable practice with a desirable one. Rather than just saying what we can't or won't do, we need to also tell ourselves what we will do. On our own, we cannot do much about global warming, political corruption, or Iraq. But we can effect positive and lasting change in our homes. By identifying and believing in our own ideas and principles, in the hidden justice in the world, in reason's ability to find it, and by teaching our children to believe in themselves, we can initiate powerful, sustainable change.

Bibliography

Aristotle, *Introduction to Aristotle*, Richard McKeon, ed. New York: Random House, 1947.

Aristotle, *Nicomachean Ethics*, Joe Sachs, translator. Newburyport, MA: Pullins Press, 2002.

Bellah, Robert N. et al., *Habits of the Heart: Individualism and Commitment in American Life*. Los Angeles: University of California Press, 1996.

Borradori, Giovanna, *Philosophy in a Time of Terror*. Chicago: University of Chicago Press, 2003.

_____ , *Philosophy in an Age of Terror: Dialogues with Jurgen Habermas and Jacques Derrida*. Chicago: University of Chicago Press, 2003.

Boyer, Ernest Jr., *A Way in the World: Family Life as Spiritual Discipline*. San Francisco: Harper & Row, 1984.

Brazelton, Terry, and Stanley Greenspan, *The Irreducible Needs of Children: What Every Child Must Have to Grow, Learn, and Flourish*. Cambridge, MA: Perseus Books, 2000.

Caputo, John, *The Prayers and Tears of Jacques Derrida: Religion without Religion*.Bloomington: Indiana University Press, 1997.

_____ , *Radical Hermeneutics: Repetition, Deconstruction, and the Hermeneutic Project*. Bloomington: Indiana University Press, 1987.

Carey, Seamus, *The Whole Child: Restoring Wonder to the Art of Parenting*. Lanham, MD: Rowman & Littlefield, 2003.

Coles, Robert, The *Moral Intelligence of Children: How to Raise a Moral Child*. New York: Random House, 1997.

Commission on Children at Risk, *Hardwired to Connect: The New Scientific Case for Authoritative Communities*. New York: Institute for American Values, 2003.

Dyer, Wayne, *Your Sacred Self: Making the Decision to Be Free*. New York: HarperCollins, 1995.

Emerson, Ralph Waldo, *Selected Essays*. New York: Penguin Books, 1984.

Erikson, Eric, *Identity and the Life Cycle*. New York: W. W. Norton and Company, 1980.

Galinsky, Ellen, *Ask the Children: The Breakthrough Study that Reveals How to Succeed at Work and Parenting*. New York: HarperCollins, 2000.

_____ , *The Six Stages of Parenthood*. Cambridge: Perseus Books, 1987.

Ginzburg, Natalia, *The Little Virtues*, Dick Davis, translator. Manchester, UK: Carcanet Press, 1985.

Greenspan, Miriam, *Healing through the Dark Emotions: The Wisdom of Grief, Fear, and Despair*. Boston: Shambhala Publications, 2003.

Guzman, Lina et. al., "How Children are Doing: The Mismatch between Public Perception and Statistical Reality." Washington, DC: Child Trends, 1999.

Heidegger, Martin, *Early Greek Thinking: The Dawn of Western Philosophy*, David Farrell Krell and Frank A. Capuzzi, translators. New York: Harper & Row, 1993.

_____ , *Basic Writings*. San Francisco: Harper & Row, 1997.

Kierkegaard, Soren, *Fear and Trembling,* Howard V. Hong and Edna H. Hong, editors and translators. Princeton, NJ: Princeton University Press, 1983.

Kindlon, Dan, *Too Much of a Good Thing: Raising Children in an Indulgent Age.* New York: Hyperion Books, 2001.

Kindlon, Dan, and Michael Thompson, *Raising Cain: Protecting the Emotional Life of Boys.* New York: Ballantine Books, 2000.

Levin, David Michael, *The Listening Self: Personal Growth, Social Change, and the Closure of Metaphysics.* New York: Routledge, 1989.

____ , *The Philosopher's Gaze: Modernity in the Shadows of Enlightenment.* Berkeley: University of California Press, 1999.

Levinas, Emmanuel, *Totality and Infinity: An Essay on Exteriority,* Alphonso Lingis, translator. Pittsburgh, PA: Duquesne University Press, 1969.

Madsen, Richard, William M. Sullivan, Ann Swidler, and Steven M. Tipton, *Individualism and Commitment in American Life.* Berkeley: University of California Press, 1985.

McKirahan, Robert, *Philosophy before Socrates: An Introduction with Text and Commentary.* Indianapolis, IN: Hackett, 1994.

McTaggart, Lynne, *The Field: The Quest for the Secret Force of the University.* New York: Quill.

Merleau-Ponty, Maurice, *The Visible and the Invisible,* A. Lingis, translator. Evanston, IL: Northwestern University Press, 1968.

Miller, Alice, *The Drama of the Gifted Child: The Search for the True Self.* New York: Basic Books, 1997.

Mohr, George J., "Psychosomatic Problems in Childhood," *Child Development* 19, no. 3 (1948): 137–142.

Nietzsche, Friedrich, *Philosophy in the Tragic Age of the Greeks,* Marianne Cowan, translator. Washington, DC: Regnery Publishing, 1998.

Norris, Kathleen, *Amazing Grace: A Vocabulary of Faith.* New York: Penguin Group, 1999.

Pipher, Mary, *Reviving Ophelia: Saving the Selves of Adolescent Girls*. New York: Ballantine Books, 1994.

Plato, *Great Dialogues of Plato*, Eric Warmington and Philip Rouse, eds. New York: Mentor Books, 1984.

Putnam, Robert, *Bowling Alone: The Collapse and Revival of American Community*. New York: Simon and Schuster, 2000.

Simmons, Rachel, *Odd Girl Out: The Hidden Aggression in Girls*. New York: Harcourt Books, 2003.

Smith, Steven, *Spinoza's Book of Life: Freedom and Redemption in the Ethics*. New Haven, CT: Yale University Press, 2003.

Spinoza, Baruch, *The Ethics and Selected Letters*. Indianapolis, IN: Hackett Books, 1982.

Tillich, Paul, *The Dynamics of Faith*. New York: Harper & Row, 1957.

———, *The Courage to Be*. New Haven, CT: Yale University Press, 1952.

Wansbrough, Henry, ed., *The New Jerusalem Bible*. New York: Doubleday, 1990.

Warren, Elizabeth, and Amelia Tyagi, *The Two-Income Trap: Why Middle-Class Mothers and Fathers Are Going Broke*. Cambridge, MA: Perseus Books, 2003.

Weinstein, Miriam, *The Surprising Power of Family Meals: How Eating Together Makes Us Smarter, Stronger, Healthier, and Happier*. Hanover, NH: Steerforth Press, 2005.

Westphal, Merold, *Transcendence and Self-Transcendence*. Bloomington: Indiana University Press, 2004.